TOO BITTER TO SWALLOW

I0491136

TOO BITTER TO SWALLOW

SAN

Notion Press

Old No. 38, New No. 6
McNichols Road, Chetpet
Chennai - 600 031

First Published by Notion Press 2016
Copyright © San 2016
All Rights Reserved.

ISBN 978-1-945579-68-4

Contents

PART-1

Preface

As far as I am concerned, the problem is solved. I have come across discussions and debates- verbal and written- and even casual arguments over the difference between a businessman and an entrepreneur. My three-year experience as a marketing man and observation and understanding as a journalist prompt me to assert that in modern context and scheme of things, an enterprising businessman and an entrepreneur are the same and indispensably linked. Because they are involved in the same process called business and both have to launch new projects, devise and adopt new methods, modes, strategies and whole lot of such initiatives to make them successful. Now there are only big and small entrepreneurs!

According to me, trade is like a coin wherein heads and tails are the same: an entrepreneur and an enterprising businessman or vice versa. Then where does the so-called traditional businessman stand? An endangered species on the brink of extinction! Nevertheless, he can retrieve his ground, provided he transforms himself into the mode of an enterprising businessman. None can prevent novel or new or modern ideas, methods, modes, styles, etc. from replacing their traditional counterparts, because that is the way of the world and life. Only those who imbibe them can survive and dominate in any world.

Segregating a businessman and an entrepreneur and granting a superior status to the latter-all these smack of a glorified bias!

Perhaps, reality is too bitter to swallow!!!

The Author

The Evolution of Trade

I can't imagine any possibility of ancient men- I mean those during Paleolithic Age, Neolithic Age, Stone Age, Copper Age and even before that –indulging in trade? Primarily because they were not ambitious, persevering, relentless, self-centred, materialistic, hell-bent and even ruthless like their modern counterparts. How could it be possible when their biological traits were in completely raw form and for the same reason the question of any sort of advancement, physical or mental, does not arise! Why? Their reasoning power hadn't matured. So the very thought of money, let alone earning and accumulating it, might not have dawned on their 'fledgling' brain.

First of all, they might have come face to face with the invincible might of natural forces like water, fire, air, sky and earth. That might have created extreme fear to the extent of obliging them to supplicate before these forces with folded hands. That might be how worship of God had taken root and spread like anything across generations that followed. Then came in hundreds, thousands and millions Gods that the people in the world worship today. The evolutionary trajectory of worship is simply astounding, considering the leaps and bounds it has made till this 21st century and the number of Gods, faiths, beliefs, isms and all sorts of divine phenomena that sprang forth.

Set aside the divine subject as that is not our concern now.

Let us scrutinize the case of trade likewise. It is within that gambit that the topic which we are going to rack our brains with- an entrepreneur and a businessman- lies.

Ancient man might have thought of purchasing goods, commodities or essentials long after his behavioural evolution. The behavioural evolution itself might have taken thousands of years in its process. First of all, the natural fire in him called hunger might have prompted him to search for food. Urge to satiate hunger might have culminated in the discovery of fire and its immense possibilities. The hunger-driven impulse might have activated even the violent and many other negative traits in him.

Maybe, this cerebral evolution led him to realization of himself, his comates, mutual interaction and its benefits and a lot more emotional and physiological streaks, which include even the need for wrapping his seat of shame. If logical evidence is anything to rely upon, behavioural and cerebral evolution eventually created in him the urge to exchange a particular type of goods or service for another. That might be how barter system came into existence and vogue.

Indus Valley civilization: Here comes the relevance of trade. When, where and why it commenced and how it meandered through civilizations and generations to reach its present status. Whatever may be the truth, historical evidence point the approving finger at the prevalence of a highly systematic drainage system and sanitary system, highly advanced transportation technology and road structure during Indus Valley civilization, arguably the oldest of all civilisations hitherto excavated. The drainage and sanitary system in those times has been equalled to that of modern Paris. Further historical evidence again prove ceramic similarities between Indus Valley civilization, Turkmenistan and Northern Iran, caravan trade between Indus Valley, Central Asia and the Iranian country and extensive network for navigation trade between Harappans and Mesopotamians. I am not going to delve deep into those aspects lest we deviate from our central subject.

Just imagine, if that civilization can boast of systems and processes, capable of holding their heads high against the most modern examples, how far those people would have gone ahead in trade and commerce! Incredibly far ahead! Drive your speculative impulse crazy at the mention of **Pushpak Viman** in the great epic poem **'Ramayan'** and the book on Aerodynamics in one of the oldest languages in the world Sanskrit and carry out an intelligent, logical and imaginative connection between all these revelations. Then you will have more than a thorough idea of all the advancements made by these people. Unfortunately, we do not have concrete evidence, but then history is built greatly on speculation, conjecture, inference, logical understanding, etc., too.

Conveniently for our guessing brains, let us suppose trade and commerce went on strong feet about 5,000 years ago. In short, trade and commerce, as we see today, is more than 5,000 years old though with a lesser technological vigour and stronger moral footing. I am sure that was not a conducive time for Radia tapes, coal scams, 2G scams and even unscrupulous politicians.

Though in no clear terms, we have already talked about trade, its evolution, progress and even the course it has taken right from ancient times to reach the present state of grandeur. Undoubtedly, trade has become the yardstick for economic development because economic vibrancy is measured in terms of trade between two and a great number of nations.

So What do you Mean by Trade?

Then what is this trade my dear? I mean the definition. What we have to keep in mind is that definitions or meanings are not iron rods and so are susceptible to change or alteration as required. In this context, I am reminded of an English poet's line- I think it is the great John Milton: "There is nothing good or bad in this world, only thinking makes it so." That means what is good for an Indian may be bad for an American and vice versa. So is the case with everybody. If right and wrong, bad and good are bound to change, why definitions can't!

Nothing in this Cosmos except the Supreme Creator or the Infinite, the Absolute, the Unknown, etc. is constant and everything is vulnerable to change, modification, alteration or amendment and even total annihilation. The most glaring example is the fact that mankind had been blindly and ignorantly believing in Solar System, envisaged by great Egyptian astronomer Ptolemy, wherein Sun revolves round the Earth and other planets until Copernicus disproved and rectified it and taught the world the present Theory of Solar System, according to which, the Earth and other planets revolve round Sun. Now, God alone knows when another Copernicus will resurrect from nowhere and modify or alter this theory.

So definitions too are bound to change according to the needs of time.

If to define simply, as per the general acceptance, trade is an exchange of goods, services, etc., between individuals, nations or so many other bodies involved for mainly monetary and related benefits. Anyway, I will define that it not only exchanges goods for money but also goodwill, cooperation and harmony among trading community and consuming community, manufacturing community and consuming community, selling community and purchasing community, etc.. And without this comprehensive and all-encompassing exchange, no trade can be qualified. Hence it can never be enhanced also. Quality is the buzzword, even in connections and relations, which in turn complements the trade potential.

We are nearing the pinpoint of our discussion: an entrepreneur and a businessman.

The most convincing example for my assertion that trade exchanges goodwill, cooperation and harmony can be noticed in the financial capital of the country itself. Supermarkets, hypermarkets and malls may come up and disappear, but you will always find those hawkers in Mumbai, employing the gift of the gab and pocketing customers and the needed money at the same spot, where you had seen him first!

How? He would have already earned the goodwill of his customers not because of his convincing or sweet tongue- of course, his tongue can create its own impact, but that is not enough-but by providing them the most wanted benefit called profit through reduced prices. He is ready to satisfy his customer by going to any extent possible within his capacity, he may even purchase his goods from clandestine markets like Chor Bazaar, Shoe Bazaar, etc., where everything, even branded goods, is damn cheap! Otherwise, how can he sell a T-shirt worth Rs 600 to Rs 900 in open market at Rs 170? That concession, even a mall-businessman cannot provide as he might have invested a heavy amount for launching his venture, let alone ordinary dealers. Not only that, they may not pursue the illegal or the 'adventurous' routes that a hawker takes.

A hawker's or an average businessman's snobbish ways can satisfy the ego of a customer, who is conscious of the fact that he is the king in modern schemes of marketing. After all, a man's greatest enemy is his own ego, just placate it and he may commit even Himalayan blunders. Mall dealer, on the other hand, with his frigid and unrealistic ways of handling people, can never create that impact.

Then you may bowl the question: what about quality? Customers in this country are aware enough to understand that quality is directly proportional to his budget; the more his budget, the better will be the quality. So, accordingly he will choose his trader and merchandise.

Ultimately, the hawker, the average businessman and the mall dealer will get what each deserves, irrespective of the rise and fall of malls and hypermarkets!

Modern Businessman and Entrepreneur are the Same!

Oxford dictionary's definition of entrepreneur goes like this: he is a person who sets up a business or businesses or production units, taking on financial and similar risks.

Obviously, this is in the hope of profit with special focus on the needs of his customer groups, which may be as expansive as a community or even a country. More often than not, he is likely to have production units also, from which he can feed his retail or wholesale venture or those of others.

If not, he will opt for local or niche-product manufacturers, bent upon getting an honourable entry into the market. Really, these 'behind-the-curtain producers' fuel up business sectors like leather, textile, gold, hardware, bakery, grocery, pharmacy, furniture, stationery, electronics, vegetables etc. And they include small-time weavers from remote and nearby places, farmers, cobblers, goldsmiths, ironsmiths, bakers and every other local artisans and workers, involved in production of various goods and items. Nowadays, this trend is catching up and such houses are mushrooming like anything to beat the tight competition from big and multi-national brands.

The dictionary's definition of businessman is as follows: he is the one who engages in business – the activity of making, buying, selling or supplying goods or services for money – especially at a high level or the one who is skilled in business and financial matters.

There is something twisty in the definition itself with immense scope for reading between the lines.

An entrepreneur is the one who sets up business and businesses. That means basically he is a businessman, then only he is graduated to an entrepreneur. That could be the only logical inference.

Then the take on risk. As if it is only the entrepreneur who takes risk and not the businessman! In modern times, at least in the case of financial risks, a businessman can be accommodated. If it is a one-man venture and not a familial continuation, he has to do it. Even the familial ventures will be forced to take that line, when financial crunch or recession-like situations starts pinching.

Or is it that the moment he takes risks, he is converted into an entrepreneur! The tendency to confine a particular quality to a specified group is not justifiable, especially the ability to take risks and come out unscathed. Even employees, affiliated to a particular organization or unit, take risks in the hope of better prospects. I think it is a part and parcel of life itself. Even the unambitious, the complacent and the smug will have to do that, though unexpectedly and against their natural disposition.

Both definitions talk about production aspect. Both the so-called entrepreneur and the businessman get entangled in production of certain, sometimes all, goods that they sell. Nowadays, this trend is catching up among businessmen and is not the prerogative of an entrepreneur any more. The businessmen who opt for this route petname those goods or merchandise as local make. This local make is nothing other than the goods of those miniscule one-man production units, run by skilled artisans or workers, with his monetary blessing.

For what all these twists and turns? Just to confuse the consumer or the customer! It is as simple as that.

According to traditional thinking, an entrepreneur and a businessman aim at profit with the means-style, ways and methods-adopted poles apart. Therein lies the crux of the matter. According to traditional school of business, an entrepreneur is innovative rather than imitative and that should have been the difference between an entrepreneur and a businessman. The entrepreneur is bound to be innovative as he wants to flow against the current and imprint the stamp of his wares on the market, and the latter imitative as he always tries to toe usual line, followed and passed on from generation to generation, and score one or two points over his rivals.

Here also there are some points which deserve a second thought. Even the course that a businessman has to chart out in modern times has to be different because of the squeezy competition that he has to encounter right from scratch. So an imitative approach will be of no use and for the same reason he needs to be innovative. So there is no point in flowing along the current and getting just the better of his competitors.

One who dabbles in trade, whether a businessman or an entrepreneur, should be enterprising- that is the right name of the game. Which means he should have or show the ability to think of new projects or new ways of doing things and make them successful. So enterprising is a natural synonym for innovative.

Again the quality by the name enterprise is not the domain of an entrepreneur, even a businessman can shape himself up in that mode. That is why experts dare to conclude that an entrepreneur should be a good or an enterprising businessman. Convincingly then, a businessman can mould himself into an entrepreneur. This is the point I am trying to prove.

That an entrepreneur and a businessman are two aspects of the same process called trade. More enterprising are the aspects, more quality products and quality services will be available in market and the trade will sparkle. In short, an enterprising businessman is as good and same as an entrepreneur. So where is the difference?

Let us imagine the process called trade as a coin with heads and tails. Both sides- entrepreneur in place of heads, enterprising businessman in place of tails- are the same. Into that coin you can incorporate, stuff, squeeze or insert the constituents called industrialists, shop-owners, jewellers, all sorts of retailers and wholesalers and the whole gamut of people involved in producing, selling, purchasing, exporting, importing, etc..

So if Ambanis and Tatas are big entrepreneurs, these enterprising businessmen are small entrepreneurs. In that situation, those who adopt traditional ways of doing business or traditional businessmen will have to pack up. Many of them have packed up, are packing up and will be doing so if they do not improve their ways and methods and transform into enterprising businessmen.

Most of the so called big entrepreneurs, whom I haven't named here, are not so by their own and sole initiative, but with the help of keen and sharp intelligence of their executive staff, to whom they owe their very existence. In fact, their only inputs are the investment and the efforts that they have put into the venture, the impulse to do business as that is the only traditional profession they have learned and the shapeless and formless dream that they have cherished without knowing the basics required for its realisation. Their expertise is only in using the intelligence of others to their advantage. One fine morning, at the spur of traditional impulse, they might have sold their whole and sole property, packed up and left for big and small cities and towns. There they flourished by dint of their ability to encash on opportunities and make use of extremely intelligent manpower.

I know one newspaper owner- sure, he can be branded as a big entrepreneur- who was so ignorant of the language that he could not understand the headline, '80-strong BJP Ministry sworn in' and suggested a change. According to him, the reader will think that the newspaper is a BJP supporter because of the word strong.

I have all my respect for small entrepreneurs or enterprising businessmen because they have transformed their 'nothingness into somethingness or even everythingness' by virtue of their own business eye, intelligence and hard work, blended with shrewdness and tricks.

Even Hawkers Could be Included in Trade!

In my opinion, even hawkers could be stuck into that coin-provided they are enterprising. After all, the devil should be given its due as authorities treat them so. I am obliged to suppose in that manner, considering the way they are being tossed and hauled to all sides in our saturated metropolises. Even they can possess or develop by own efforts the quality called enterprise and become an entrepreneur , launching new projects and adopting novel methods and initiatives. Why not? Watch and learn how they outsmart the cops and civic officials with greasy palms, capable of attracting green notes as swiftly as opposite poles of a magnet, emerge safe and continue their business for years at the same spot and in the same furtive and sneaky manner. All metropolises, especially Mumbai, are stark witnesses to this strange phenomenon. Some of them may even transfigure into enterprising businessmen or entrepreneurs. In fact, real examples are there of hawkers transforming into big entrepreneurs worth billions. A skim through Middle East trade history can provide many examples. For most of them, Mumbai was a launching pad. A particular story is the one of a tender-coconut hawker, who went on to become one of the biggest retailers in Middle East. It is heard that the front portion of his house in the state of Kerala is always dotted with BMWs and Mercedes Benzes.

Take a look at the history of great entrepreneurs, dazzling in the global economic firmament, and you may come across those who have risen to the present pinnacle from the thorny lap of penury and financial helplessness.

As Lord Byron has said, truth is always stranger than fiction!

Selling is an art. Americans are known to be the best salesmen as they are capable of selling refrigerators even in freezing Iceland. Imagine yourself to be a marketing man. If your boss holds out two different brands of the same product, of course, of different prices, which one you will choose to sell? The cheaper or the costlier one? In my opinion, the best salesman is the one who chooses the costlier one as he will have to sweat it out and need all tactics in the world to market it. The cheaper one is an easy option as price factor is too alluring for a customer.

Surely, only a good salesman can be a good businessman. Then in no uncertain terms only a good or enterprising businessman can be an entrepreneur.

Remember, purchasing too is an art because if your sense of judgment goes wrong, your pocket too will get drained. Try your luck at Fashion Street in Mumbai!

As business mainly constitutes purchasing and selling, an entrepreneur too has to source out his income through these activities. Then what all this fuss is about? An entrepreneur must be a good or enterprising businessman and it is ridiculous to segregate both and treat one as superior.

Here is a Traditional Businessman!

Let us now spotlight the difference between a traditional businessman and an enterprising businessman or an entrepreneur.

Traditional wisdom advises that one should feel the pulse of time and do accordingly. For the same reason, a traditional businessman observes, even conducts a personal feasibility study of the current trends, sets his various plans and executes them accordingly. He cannot even think of new methods and styles, unless prodded by demands of the situation, just because he is not in the habit of taking risk. In fact, maybe, he is afraid of it like the devil at the sight of a crucifix.

For example, let us just visualize what a traditional businessman does if he stumbles upon the idea of embarking on a business venture as common as textile.

The traditional businessman, wasting no time – time and tide wait for no man – evaluates the potential of the venture that he wishes to step into, the capital required, the ways and means by which money can be raked in and a whole lot of such possibilities and carries out the task. It goes without saying that he would have undergone several brain-racking minutes with men who matter, including his kith and kin, venture capitalists, Chartered Accountants etc. And within no time his brainchild turns into a reality as he gets all the required back-up.

The fact is that, maybe, he stumbles upon the idea by sheer expediency of the need to retain the family tradition and embraces it reluctantly or willingly-again that willingness is suspect since it will be quite evident from his initial mannerisms in that garb. This is because many traditional businessmen are so not by intuition or instinct or enthusiasm-enthusiasm may play its role in rare cases-but because of familial necessity or compulsion or many such hazy reasons.

The Unscrupulous lot Among Them!

Of course, there are guys among this traditional stuff who count the chickens before they are hatched and the consequent rosy life they can lead. Commitment to the society or the people in general is nowhere in their dictionary. Ethical business is indeed a great marvel, but they want money and earn it by hook or crook.

But the fact of the matter is that public is not an ass anymore. The pearls of wisdom, flowing into their cerebrum through TV, Internet and a huge number of electronic and digital gadgets and media, are difficult to control and this process improves his intellectual capacity and enables him to distinguish between good quality and bad quality. He is not like his yesteryear counterparts, who get carried away by the ability to convince that marketing professionals, advertisement gurus etc., are endowed with, only to be taken for a stupid ride.

For some, ethics is a taboo in business and their deeds will have that tinge throughout until they come across the pitfalls and get doomed. To be frank and fair to the system, this 'some' was in majority at one time, in exactly brute majority except those with entrepreneurial stuff and capable of realizing the 'make or break' ability of the customer, who can enrich or pauperise them in a jiffy. One can observe that phenomenon in the markets every day. Yesterday's kings are falling like hell from grace at the feet of penury and, maybe, eking out a desperate existence.

An Entrepreneur or an Enterprising Businessman is Born!

Yet another basic difference between a traditional businessman and an entrepreneur or an enterprising businessman: an entrepreneur is born and a traditional businessman is moulded due to familial necessity, traditional occupation, expediency or many such flimsy grounds.

In my opinion, if the guy is with an in-born flair for business, he deserves to be called an entrepreneur, because, in all probability, he will follow in similar footsteps.

What are these footsteps? My earlier paragraphs have been throwing light on the modalities of traditional business culture – the way business was being done in markets by those traditional businessmen, whom I want to differentiate from entrepreneurs. Why? Because there is a yawning gap between the two, firstly, due to the fact that an entrepreneur is born rather than moulded by circumstances and secondly, he is born with flair, embellished with bright ideas that in turn will bring him and the customers only good in plenty, as his methods are customer-friendly. That aspect fortifies his customer base, because of the abundant goodwill and the great trust-quotient that he earns.

The way he utilizes the resources at his disposal is far-reaching, even path-breaking, worthy to be emulated by the Lilliputians in the trade. As everybody in this space age would love to believe, short-term benefits are of no use for any businessman, traditional or enterprising, to establish himself in the field. He has to expand his customer-base, for that he should earn their goodwill, which will end up in great trust quotient. These sublime qualities come with a price on his part. He has to fulfil their wish-list or needs through the delivery of quality goods and quality services.

This is one of the most important tricks of trade that a traditional businessman can freely learn from an entrepreneur or an enterprising businessman.

Most of the traditional businessmen follow what their counterparts in earlier times would do. Squeeze out the maximum from the employees by doling out the minimum.

Modern staffers are too intelligent for such nasty tricks. Obviously, the minimum doles will only demoralize him and he is bound to give his worst. At the end of the day, it is the employer who is going to lose.

According to me, the best businessman or an enterprising businessman is the one who takes out the best from his employees; when you give him the best in the form of good treatment and perks, he will provide the best in return. That will reflect in the quality of his output. So effectively, when the business and businessman grows, the employee must grow. The net result: a harmonious growth, encompassing one and all, including the customer-base. A traditional businessman will be well advised to remember that in earlier times, choices were very few for employees, now the options are too many that sometimes aspirants get confounded with confusion. If that reality is not accepted, he will have to face the harsh music that entails with his short-sighted strategies.

An entrepreneur or an enterprising businessman can guide the traditional businessman in this aspect too as he is a master in it. That is how he slowly and successfully expands his empire of outreach.

Ultimately, there is no alternative left for me except to say that a traditional businessman sees his human resource as a tool to climb up the ladder of growth, whereas an entrepreneur treats them as his peers or colleagues to increase the productivity of his enterprise. Simultaneously, their productivity and quality of life will also enhance.

That is why being innovative has an edge over being imitative. This is the reason why an entrepreneur or an enterprising businessman is miles apart from a traditional businessman.

Transform Yourself into an Entrepreneur!

One doesn't need to think twice to conclude that a traditional businessman has to transfigure himself into the mode of an entrepreneur, if he wants to touch the sky in his trade zone or even survive. Too many brands, companies, enterprises and firms under the garb of manufacturing, marketing, consultancy, servicing, banking, etc., are clogging the market just like vehicles in traffic snarl-ups. In that scenario, if the traditional businessman continues with his brash and reckless ways in dealing with his customers, employees, dealers and others, only time can decide what his situation will be. Delicate, diplomatic and cultured handling of customers, dealers and employees is imperative and it will make all the difference so as to enable him to survive the onslaught of the tight competition.

Take a leaf from an entrepreneur's or an enterprising businessman's book, try out once and experience the result. That will give an idea as how he succeeds in this zone.

Generally speaking, flair, innate or not, for selling is enough to see a businessman through the cut-throat or merciless competition, wherein every Tom, Dick and Harry is at each other's belly to get the better of each and everyone. After all, selling is the earning part of a businessman whether he is traditional or enterprising, because purchases or production are his main inputs. This process is at his mercy and he has to be discreet in his interactions so as to come out not only unscathed but also in flying colours.

Beware of this Dangerous Salesman Fraternity!

"Oh, my end-user is customer and I have to gratify him only." If a complacent or an overbearing traditional businessman (experience teaches us that they are of that frame of mind) tends to think in this line and rests assured that he is going to reap a big harvest in the form of sales, he is in a fool's paradise. He is unaware of the great danger potential of his employees, who are nothing but his conduit or his passage to the so-called customers. This conduit or link can collude with wily lot among the customers, interested in extracting their pound of flesh. They too have a die-hard faith in the minimum-input-and-maximum-output strategy, which means through one rogue staffer, the customer can get away with double or treble or even four times the worth of the cost he pays. The ubiquitous company representatives will always be at their squeezing best and by their diplomatic and cunning ways will take away yet another chunk. Again, an unsuspecting and overconfident traditional businessman may write off the loss as chicken feed. He can't afford that even, because millions and billions of drops make an ocean.

I am talking about the great salesman fraternity, pivotal in helping business empires make leaps and bounds. A businessman, traditional or enterprising, with his capacity only to manage limited zones of activity cannot achieve such astronomical advantages. For that huge achievement, he will have to use the salesman as his crutch. Of course, in a way and convincingly so, the key to a businessman's success is in the hands of salesmen. And it is indispensably essential to keep him in good humour. This may be the trickiest of all tricks of the trade. So many business empires have collapsed as they failed to cater to the needs of this group of labour.

This clandestine reciprocity goes unhindered in small and big retail and wholesale enterprises of everything under the sun, even hotels and similar eateries. However, malls with strict price tag, supply system and surveillance network are an exception. So we can assume, actual truth can be anybody's guess.

How Entrepreneurs or Enterprising Businessmen Treat Them!

As the entrepreneur treats the workforce like salesmen, sales executives or in total the marketing personnel as peers or colleagues and fills their cup of happiness in the form of handsome remuneration and perks, they are a happy lot and give their best to the boss.

Let us take the case in point of the state of Kerala, which stands out from the rest in the country for being solely a consuming market. Production-wise, nothing substantial happens in this land of Ayurveda, Kathakali and Mohiniyattam. However, much to the chagrin of dejected moneybags, who want to tap its huge potential but fails to do so because of the hugely demanding labour force, the state boasts of huge retail and wholesale business houses of gold, textiles, cars, hardware, music and I tell you everything that a human mind can imagine. You cannot witness that kind of hugeness even in the financial capital of the country, Mumbai. Retail outlets of 10,000 and more square feet are galore in this 'city state.' Now, just conjecture an idea of the possible extremely tight situation in its markets, because of the huge number of towns that it has. Posh and even luxurious when compared to the quaint – not for their palaces or havelis, because of their 'ancient' look due to lack of modernity – and impoverished ones in other states. You can call them cities as in the case of corporations, municipal towns in the case of municipalities, village towns in the case of panchayats of A, B and C grades. The unflinching doomsayers are at a loss to explain away the pace with which these cities, municipal towns and village towns march ahead. Even B and C grade villages are wearing an advanced look with their posh townships.

My point here is that even with an average common sense one can imagine the large number of brands, companies, products – all consumer and other types of goods of all grades and qualities- that throng these markets. It is a virtual marketing chaos. Anyway, the customer is spoilt for choice, such is the pandemonium of goods and brands. What will that mediocre, average and, at the most, reasonably good businessman with his traditional ways of selling do? There is no point in panicking! You have to take the bull by its horns and not the tail. You can't think of running away from reality at this crucial and critical juncture.

Entrepreneurship or Enterprise Must for Survival!

Here is the relevance of entrepreneurship or enterprise and that is the point I want to drive home. It is here a traditional businessman's metamorphosis or transformation into an entrepreneur or enterprising businessman is unavoidably essential. Otherwise, with the obsolete methods, he will be forced to shut shop and pack up. He has to forget about his traditional ways, rather he should devise new ways, methods, styles and strategies and deal with the daunting challenges ahead. Of course, his rivals also will do the same as he can't underestimate their potential. Then it will be a war of strategies, methods, ways and styles of countless stakeholders. The war for spoils of business will be on and on without any stop. By this time, the traditional businessman should have turned into the mood and mode of an entrepreneur. He should be habituated to taking risks. He must convince and cajole his workforce into giving out their best. He should be monitoring his customers' requirements and catering to them with all heart and soul. Quality maintenance must be his utmost priority. A complete reversal of strategies and resultant fortunes can also be witnessed if everything reaches its logical conclusion.

Inevitably, this war of the daring and dashing will however have an end. The victors will keep ruling the roost, wearing the mantle of success, and continue their triumphal onward march. The vanquished will definitely vanish from the markets. How it happens?

It is this war for dominance that creates sales and promotion campaigns, rebates and discounts, freebies, sales melas, festival sales and such gimmicks, all with the motive of luring the customer. Hundreds of ideas might have sprouted in the brains of these warring professionals. Successful ideas will survive and the unsuccessful ones will be erased forever. Businessmen with successful ideas are the victors and those with unsuccessful Ideas are the vanquished. Moreover, ideas that have borne fruit will be imitated by one and all and they will continue their success stories for years to come.

As time passes by another set of ideas, aimed at achieving success, will take shape and replace the older ones. Traditional businessmen and entrepreneurs may come and go, but this cycle will go on forever.

Nothing more is required to prove the dominance of an entrepreneur over a traditional businessman.

Redefine Industry and Entrepreneurship!

According to traditional perception, retailing or for that matter wholesaling too, is the zone earmarked for the class called businessmen and manufacturing and other production-based zones for entrepreneurs. There are some who indulge in both. If you are going to classify someone as entrepreneur in accordance with the huge size of his enterprise and the astronomical turnover he records, sorry my dear, you will have to apply the same yardstick for those basking in retail sector also. There are giants here not only in global arena, even in our largest democracy of the world like Lulu group and many other Titans with spacy and swanky malls and hypermarkets. Worse, even the manufacturing and production sector giants like Tatas, Birlas and Reliance have already embarked upon this zone and are making their presence felt.

It is high time that we improved our definition of industry. I will define industry as a process or a unit or an enterprise that is productive – in other terms, something that provides job or employment, even if it provides job only for one person. Truly, small and huge production units or enterprises qualify for that status as they provide employment in large numbers. Now, the so-called experts will have to add retailing and wholesaling sector to that category as they too provide employment in large numbers, both direct and indirect.

What is an industry? Let us see how dictionary explains that word. According to Oxford Advanced Learner's Dictionary, it is the production of goods from raw materials, especially in factories or in providing a particular service. And the Concise Oxford English Dictionary goes on to add: an economic activity concerned with the processing of raw materials and manufacture of goods in factories or a particular branch of economic or commercial activity.

What About Health Sector!

Does this mean health sector, which comprises hundreds and thousands of hospitals, both government-run and private, small and big clinics, small and big laboratories with their own existence and identity, is not an industry? Of course, there is no processing of raw materials or production of goods. Instead, you see hundreds and thousands of employees like doctors, nurses, radiographers, lab technicians, lab assistants, etc., indulging or involved in humanitarian services, whose end-product is nothing but relief or recovery for patients when they are cured of their minor, major and dreaded diseases. Some of them are a match to the production industry giants in size, turnover and the enormity of human capital they invest. And with same or most of the times bigger salary structure. Or what more you need to call that sector an industry!

And Education Sector!

What about the education sector? The large or even huge number of arts colleges, science colleges, engineering colleges, medical colleges, technical institutes, agricultural colleges, hotel management institutes, universities, technology institutes, science - law - medical academies and the whole range of institutions coming under that tag

SAN

throughout the country too dole out employment. And they produce scholars, Ph Ds, doctors, doctorates, engineers, teachers, industrial experts, economists, business executives, scientists, moralists, experts in all sorts of matters, bankers, politicians and the whole ilk of professionals. And never ever dare to think these personalities are would-be Toms, Dicks and Harris. They are the future of this great nation with great culture and greater traditions, around whom this nation will revolve and clinging on to whose coat-tails it will propel to unimaginable glory. Are they not equal to the so-called production giants? A fact quite evident from the way they branch out in different directions within the country. They too are good and even better pay-masters. Then what's the problem? Will not these credentials suffice to be branded as an industry!

Do not industrialise education! This may be the thunder likely to emanate from hypocritical moralists and politicians. When they claim that in so many states primary and secondary education is free, politicians or moralists are aware that this facility is financed by the respective governments. How? Utilising the tax-payers' money available with the governments in millions and billions and, mind you, these tax-payers include even parents of children for whose education the money is diverted. In a way governments make use of their money for their own education! Is that free education? Moreover, how education can become only a service and not an industry as none in that field does their duty for free! It is a service sector or service industry! Here too quality counts!

And the Hospitality Sector!

If both the sectors-health and education- mentioned above are ignored and belittled, it is not surprising that the hospitality sector, which constitutes seven-star, five-star, three-star, two-star and single star hotels that cater to the needs of the rich and the extravagant- their pockets and egos are always puffed with green notes and pride respectively- then middle class, low-class and mediocre hotels with homely and mouth-watering delicacies that quench the thirst and hunger of ordinary people like me and the resorts with innumerable tags and specialities, is enjoying the same peripheral status.

In a socially developed state like Kerala, where according to the World Bank, villages are vanishing and turning into towns – this process is on way to completion, it is expected- this sector is hugely job-potential and you can see all kinds of star hotels, all genres of middle class, low-class and mediocre hotels and palatial and cosy resorts dotting the whole length and breadth of the state. And just examine the wages that they dish out to their employees. Mind-boggling even when compared to the so-called industrialized states like Gujarat and Maharashtra and far ahead when contrasted with the national average. Other states like Tamil Nadu, Punjab, Karnataka, Andhra Pradesh, etc., whose governments accept and acknowledge the presence of villages and the need for their progress, you will find this sector thriving like nowhere.

Catering: In several states like Kerala, this sector has undergone diversification. Fortunately or unfortunately, the trend of outsourcing has cut into this sector and catering sector is carrying out that task at its own will, conditions, rules and regulations.

Traditionally, marriage had always been a great occasion for relatives, kith and kin, near and dear ones to come together for an emotional or familial expression of love and care. In those days- I am talking about my college days- there never used to be a shortage of kith and kin since the usual norm was minimum four or five children for a parental couple. All these near and dear ones speak their hearts out and even cook the required delicacies with mutual cooperation and coordination. Lots of love and affection, showered on the occasion, are likely to be reflected in the flavour of the cuisine. That good old memory is a luxury now, in fact, the rarest of all rarities. In the initial stage, famous restaurants or hotels would carry out the task as they were supposed to be well-versed in the art of cooking.

Now, that trend is almost gone; a new generation of entrepreneurs or enterprising businessmen with more than enough ambition and expertise, has emerged. They have their own cooks, serving people, dish-washers, tea-brewers etc.. On the fixed day, these entrepreneurs make a planned and calculated entry with their staffers and paraphernalia and carry out the whole task swiftly and efficiently, much to the satisfaction of all players involved. Direct and indirect employment is created in abundance.

Still, both these sectors are far behind in getting an emphatic industry status.

My Goodness, Even Banking Sector!

Then comes the cash-rich banking sector that is responsible for the millions and billions of rupees flowing into Indian markets in the form of Gross Domestic Product or GDP. Branches in hundreds and thousands of various banks have fanned out, courtesy to the ambitious individuals and organizations, who want to spread their wings by branching out in various parts of the country. In number itself they are astronomical. The number of employees too comes in the same category. With handsome remuneration and perks, they stand taller above their peers in other sectors and I have heard they are the cynosure of all parental eyes that look for suitable partners for their beloved daughters. They have such venerable social status and are more than high in their standard of living.

Still our experts are reluctant to dole out an unambiguous industry status to this sector!

Construction Sector Too!

Another victim of such an expert apathy is none other than the construction sector, wherein hundreds and thousands of buildings in the form of houses, hypermarkets, supermarkets, shopping complexes, shopping malls, hospitals, etc., are coming up in the form of even skyscrapers and sold for unimaginable prices that skyrocket disproportionately and end up like fairytales for listeners. Things have come to such a pass that a 400 or 600-square feet I BHK (1 bedroom, hall, and kitchen) flat costs minimum Rs 55 lakh in the city of Mumbai and has become a dream for laymen or ordinary men who eke out a meagre existence. The startling fact is that nobody is complaining or carping at anybody and everybody is satisfied with the dream of a huge sum, likely to earn when the property is sold. That possibility is a far cry, in view of the fact that a Mumbai local is rooted inextricably to the pulse and impulse of the city to survive at any cost, irrespective of financial, geographical, climatic, social, communal or any such catastrophes.

In one of the most populated countries in the world like our's, where the population has crossed one-billion mark and is still counting, one doesn't need an extra fertile brain to surmise the innumerable buildings likely to crop up and the human resource to be involved in such ventures. That itself will give an ample idea of the money-flow into that sector and its potential for employment- generation. The owners of some of these conglomerates are counted among the richest men in this country. The wages too are above ordinary and capable of attracting even extremely skilled labourers, masons, carpenters, artisans etc. Then what inhibits these experts from tagging the sector with the elusive status called industry!

The reason that experts are likely to cite is the 'floating' nature of the human capital that makes up the sectors like hospitality, catering and construction. So what! Which industry now does not boast of 'floating' employees, who keep on skipping form one company or group to another as per the fatness of offers that they get! Nowadays, all the policies devised by the governments are in favour of employers, who believe in the theory of maximum labour from minimum wages or maximum benefits from minimum wages. Hire and fire is the usual mantra in the industrial circles. Security and permanency in jobs is an old and obsolete usage. Better to forget such cosy situations as they are equal to pipe-dreams, hence the human-capital drain from one enterprise to another.

How can that condition prevent experts from imparting the 'great' industry status to these sectors? Of course, sectors like education, health and banking are better placed as far as permanence of the employees is concerned. Even they are denied an emphatic industry status by experts for reasons only known to them!

If to return to the main point of our discussion, are these institutions, hospitals, IITs, arts and science colleges, laboratories, star hotels, nationalized and scheduled banks, skyscrapers, magnetic mansions or palatial buildings, new catering firms, etc., not the exemplary proofs of entrepreneurship? Are brains behind these monumental institutions, organizations and structures, not enterprising businessmen or entrepreneurs, who employ new methods, styles and means to propagate their service and thus create opportunities in hundreds and thousands?

Definitely, Trade is an Industry!

Definitely, whether the media experts, who enjoy hammering down into the nation's throat any nonsense that they are convinced of, digest it or not, trade is an industry since it generates direct and indirect jobs in hundreds and thousands in several cities and towns of this country and hence is highly productive. This is not an invention of mine, but a truth that has been strutting around and maybe, the so-called experts failed to notice.

You do not have to go far, just go on a tour to South of the country- the Golden South as one of the English TV channels has pet named it- and observe the textile, gold and diamond, grocery, stationery, leather, hardware and paint, electronics and many such business establishments. You will marvel at some of those huge, plush and expensive showrooms with the latest decorative items and digital operative systems, stunning display of wares and obliging salesmen, saleswomen and other staffers, lined up to satisfy customers' purchase - related needs.

What a Breath-Taking Transformation!

Twenty or 25 years ago, this was not the case. The pattern of trade, both retail and wholesale, has undergone a breath-taking transformation! How it became possible?

Maybe, the overall development by means of high social development as a consequence of high human resource development and equally high economic development, that certain states like Kerala witnessed-among all states in the country, Kerala has arguably the lowest urban-rural disparity- turned the whole scenario around. *(DETAILS IN PART II)*

The resultant upswing in purchasing capacity saw the flow of various brands into the market. In fact, floodgates were opened. Imported goods are not a luxury now due to its ubiquitous presence in white and black markets. The customer is now virtually baffled as he finds himself indecisive over the choice, because of the multiplicity of brands in markets. Of course, metropolitan cities, on its own accord, were bound to experience such upswing and bafflement with the huge population count and the consequent potential.

This is the situation right now, I can vouch for South of the country, especially Kerala. The market potential is with its antenna up and ahead, so is the customer base. Everybody is out to grab major chunk of this market and customer base and putting in his best efforts, both in quality and quantity.

Unlike in the past, every sector- textile, gold and diamond, grocery, stationery, leather, hardware and paint, electronics and many such business options- is spreading its wings or branching out and entering every city, municipal and village town markets, come what may, in the hope of grabbing its chunk.

Mere entry into these cities and towns is not going to bring them the fortune that they yearn for. In the face of stifling competition, they are employing novel methods and strategies to outwit their immediate and other competitors or rivals and capture major chunk of spoils at stake.

The net result: a new generation of enterprising businessmen or entrepreneurs with lots of innovation and invention has appeared on the business arena. They have the same financial might as production or manufacturing giants and are providing employment in thousands with equally high salaries and perks. In fact, in my perspective, this is the beginning of a retail revolution, wherein the way the business is being done hitherto is undergoing a significant transformation.

The New Textile World!

The case in point here is textile business. There are great number of big retailers in South of the country and I am citing the example of one Kalyan Textiles, based at Thrissur in Kerala. The firm has 25 showrooms in Kerala, Tamil Nadu, Karnataka and Middle East, served by about 6,000 or 8,000 employees. Big and fiscally strong like a manufacturing boss with several units and 6,000 or 8,000 employees under his control! Many of its rivals in Kerala and the whole of South may have almost the same fiscal power and maybe, less number of branches here and there. How does it pull on in such a suffocating situation? How does it manage to overcome the competition from rivals due to various brands, both Indian and multi-national, etc.? It is here tricks of trade will come into action!

It is heard, the enterprising boss in question did not cower behind the mountain-like competition and dared to contact expert weavers in the whole country, especially Kancheepuram and Benares, and has succeeded in making them spin the yarn and fabric of his own choice, design, pattern and several such specifications. Now Kalyan itself is a brand, flying high and outsmarting all other brands, including Indian and multi-national, in its zone of influence and goodwill.

As far as production side here is concerned, this revolution has brought into focus and life many farmers, cobblers, goldsmiths, ironsmiths, bakers and every other local artisan, who are ready to sway to the business-related whims and fancies of several bosses with control over various sectors like leather, textile, gold, hardware, bakery, grocery, furniture, electronics, vegetables, etc.. These farmers or craftsmen would otherwise have sunk into oblivion or misery for lack of opportunities.

It was known that Lulu's own outlet in the spacious and fabulous Lulu Mall at Kochi had entered into a pact with many farmers, who matter, for exclusive supply of their vegetable produce, before the enterprise set its tone in Kochi. Reliance Fresh too had launched this kind of profit-oriented measure, when it set its foot in Kochi about 10 or 15 years ago.

Definitely, Kalyan's rivals might have followed suit and adopted various methods, modes and advantageous measures like own fashion shows to improve their prospects. Then one can straightaway assume that a large number of small production units with a managing weaver at the helm of its affairs and some of his colleagues as assistants, may have mushroomed at various weaving centres in the country, realising designs, colours, patterns and the whole range of specifications of these textile bosses. My goodness! Just imagine the mind-boggling and unimaginable situation that customers, who are kings in modern scheme of marketing, would find themselves in. Brands galore to dazzle their eyes and brain and lift them to dizzying heights of delight and satisfaction!

And also one can make out the number of employees being protected and taken care of by these showrooms and their bosses. Numberwise itself the employment potential is as huge and beneficial as a manufacturing unit. What more proofs you need to establish that trade is an industry!

One should see the showrooms. In fact, that itself is enough to entice our customers, who get easily pepped up by the very appearance of showrooms. Nine-storeyed showroom with each floor measuring 10,000 square feet, four-storeyed outlet with each floor having a space of 30,000 square feet, two-storeyed shop with each floor as spacy as 50,000 square feet- many of the textile outlets that dot various cities and towns of Kerala and Tamil Nadu are as huge and capable of satisfying their rich and extravagant customers, who are prepared to go to any extent for their favourite brands, designs, patterns, etc..

This is Entrepreneurship!

I think new or novel strategies, ideas, modes, styles related to marketing are born every day and flow into the market by practice and imitation. Imitated strategies get scrapped as fast as possible. That is business and this is the reason why creativity has become as important as merchandises. This is only commercial creativity and in no way it is linked to artistic or literary creativity, remember that!

In future marketing scenario, delivery at your doorstep is going to be a common norm. Already, online and some offline companies have ventured to do so and are reaping advantages. Door-to-door canvassing and selling is a usual thing in villages now.

If these strategists are not entrepreneurs, whom are you going to call entrepreneurs or enterprising businessmen? I am again and emphatically driving home my point that any businessman deserves to be called an entrepreneur provided he is enterprising and so capable of employing new methods and strategies to take forward his enterprise successfully. And I can dish around so many examples.

This phenomenon is not restricted to only textiles my dear! It cuts across all sectoral lines and includes even medical shops, which face leg-pulling competition from Ayurveda system of medicine, flaunting not only its comprehensive curing methods and natural ingredients, but also cosmetic creativity!

Golden Sharks are Pioneers!

Gold or jewellery is another sector that is giving birth to such enterprising businessmen or entrepreneurs. In reality, they should be given the credit for pioneering this mode of business and showing the world how they can be as successful as manufacturing units.

From where else you can choose examples for this kind of entrepreneurship than Kerala, which purchases, as per a survey, 15 percent of the total gold consumed by the whole country? If I am not wrong, Alukas group and Kalyan group are pioneers in fanning out into cities, municipal and village towns and tapping the huge potential therein. There were veterans earlier too, who relegated themselves to the status of traditional businessmen without the ability to take risk and spread their empire and thus conquer zones of productivity and potential! In those times, Thrissur was one of the best retail markets for gold in the country. Even then these traditional stuffs hesitated to take the plunge much to their disadvantage. Some of them have already been eased out from the business horizon itself!

I think these golden sharks are the best paymasters by virtue of the prodigious amount of business they get from the extremely vibrant market of Kerala itself. I have read in national dailies, published from Mumbai, that minimum Rs 1,000 crore worth gold is being smuggled to Kerala from Dubai every month or so. That is the black market, so white market can go as far as you surmise!

There is an underlying reason behind this. Do not think that Keralites want to see their wives draped in gold ornaments. One may tend to think so while witnessing the roaring business these swanky or plush outlets do. I have even doubted whether my countrymen have included gold in their diet!

It is Keralite's business eye that induces him to go for a major purchasing spree. Half of the dowry, of astronomical worth, is always transferred by means of gold ornaments. That is what bridegrooms here always demand from bride's family and the latter has no objection in obliging. Why? Because for husbands, it is an asset. During the time of fiscal crisis or if they embark upon any new undertaking or business, they can pledge these ornaments and take loan. Outlets for such 'golden' options are innumerable here! Even they branch out dear! Take the example of Manappuram and Muthoot and count the number of branches!

Sure, they are among the best paymasters in the trade and the salary and perks these golden sharks are willing to shell out include food and accommodation, as was the previous custom in Middle East. So the local boy or man, working as a salesman or an executive with that much salary and perks in his homeground, will be more than happy and satisfied. It is heard that like bank staffers, they too are in great pull in marriage market.

Moreover, the number of showrooms depends upon the inclination of these bosses to spread out their empire. It is heard one of the leading groups has as many as 125 branches in the whole country and Middle-East. Then definitely - if to opt for a rough calculation- it will have 7,000 employees. Most of these golden bosses have branched out in South of the country- even in Mumbai and New Delhi- then their and the yellow metal's favourite haunt Middle-East. Each of them will be having minimum 10 branches- arguably the lowest number. So - if I am not wrong in my guesswork- these 10 branches should be utilising services of at least 500 or more employees. That is the employment-potential of these outlets and it is as high as manufacturing or production units. How many more proofs are essential to assert that trade is also an industry?

These brightly lit and plush-and-extravagant-looking outlets with liveried salesmen and staffers cosying up to neat, clean and sometimes gaudy- mainly female – customers are indeed a soothing sight to behold. Gold prices may or may not slump, rubber or coconut prices may or may not crash, cash-crop prices like those of spices may sink or may not sink, that is not a botheration for these golden sharks because their business will be as alive as before. This is quite clear from the fact that most of the popular TV programmes will always be sponsored by these jewellery groups. This is indicative of the charming spell that the yellow metal casts on Keralites! The sole reason may be that it comes to their rescue during hard and stifling times!

Now, where will these entrepreneurs go for designs, patterns and specifications concerning ornaments they prefer? Whom they will seek out for that job? Herein comes the question of indirect employment and its beneficiaries! They are none other than craftsmen or artisans, dealing with ornamental designs. Here too it is anybody's guess that each of these golden bosses will have his own designing units under the control of one chief craftsman and his assistants. The number of designing units need not be same as that of branches. And these craftsmen may not be carrying out their role under one roof. It is heard most of these artisans execute the designing work at home, far from the supervising eyes of their bosses though under their 'monetary grace.'

Most of them are likely to be goldsmiths or such trained personnel, who are experts in 'extracting' gold too. According to an old saying, each stroke of a goldsmith is equal to a very minute granule that splinters out in the twinkling of an eye from the main piece. Fortunately, it is invisible to normal eyes. For the same reason, when he winds up the day's work and sweeps clean the floor of his workshop, just imagine the number of such minutest granules that can catch the goldsmith's 'magnified' sight and the extra 'gold' he can pocket. This is the marvel and wealth 'etched' with this job for a discerning and ambitious artisan!

Electronics is Toeing the Same Line!

Electronics is another sector, wherein entrepreneurial skills and employment-potential, matching any manufacturing boss and his unit respectively, are on display. Some of the showrooms like Bismi Electronics give the impression of a mall or a hypermarket. Rightly, you will feel so when you step into these showrooms. Its ambience is just electrifying and mesmerising, because before your eyes is the electronics universe, replete with televisions of latest model and technology like LED or smart TV, washing machines with the latest technology and model in look, shape and all, then fans, refrigerators, air-conditioners, home appliances and all devices and gadgets that are most modern in look, shape and model. Salesmen and staffers, in large numbers and ready to appear at your beck and call to satisfy your needs and requirements, will remind you of the enormity of a manufacturing unit without the ear-piercing effect that men and machines make.

This sector is also spreading its roots in the hope of taking advantage of the business potential at stake. Houses that do not have modern electronic devices and gadgets and even computers are very few and this explains why these dealers branch out their concerns. Major players in the field have already ensured their presence in important cities and towns. Everyone is eyeing and vying for the topmost slot by throwing money in torrents and adopting strategies for capturing major chunk of the customer base and the consequential market. They too may be having technicians under their control, with high electrical sense and less qualification, who can design and assemble several such gadgets that can be sold or marketed with a 'local-make' tag, as several other sectors do, to ease competition.

The New Automobile World is Huge, Productive!

According to my perception, automobile dealership cum service is another sector that has the potential for entrepreneurship and employment generation on a large scale. These dealership cum service centres are worthy of note or elaborate explanation. Kerala is possibly the best market for Maruti and Toyota brands since both companies' biggest dealers are in this 'industrially backward' land! According to a report in India's highest circulated commerce daily, Kochi is increasingly becoming the biggest or the most potential market for Audis, BMWs and Mercedes Benzes. This shows the state's market scope for hi-fi cars and even 'middle-of-the-road' cars of modern technology and good condition like Maruti brands, Toyota brands, Tata brands, Chevrolet brands, etc.

I think all cars of 'modern technology and good condition' have their dealership and service centres in almost all cities and municipal towns, including district headquarters and even village towns. The number of cities, district headquarters and municipal towns in the state will add to minimum 114 (my calculation is possibly wrong since it is a random one). Taking into consideration only 'middle-of-the-road' cars, minimum number of centres that cover these cities and towns should be $114 \times 3 = 342$. The moot-point here is the personnel that these centres deploy to execute their automobile tasks. Even if you are going to suppose the average number of employees as 50 at each centre, the total count comes to about 17,100 (again this figure of mine is likely to be stupendously wrong because there may be showrooms that accommodate 300 or 400 or 500+ employees each).

Like the Toyota showroom at Kochi-the biggest display of Toyota cars and its service possibilities not only in the country but also Asia. Another 7-storeyed, hi-tech, monumental, huge, majestic, fabulous, imposing, enormous, magnificent–you take the help of all adjectives in English language that impart the same sense and still it will not suffice-structure or building to amaze at! All Toyota showrooms and service centres across the state are owned by a single man! The aforementioned showroom itself may have personnel strength of 1,000. So the number of employees taken care of by this employer through all his Toyota showrooms in the state should be at least 8,000. Is not this enterprise as big as a manufacturing unit? What is the problem then in accepting trade as an industry!

The Furniture World is Fabulous!

Furniture is another business option that deserves a special description. This section mainly deals with wooden furniture that grows in tandem with construction and real estate sector. Construction of houses, malls, hypermarkets, supermarkets, shopping complexes, etc., will entail the necessity of furniture of all shades, hues, raw materials and specifications that owners want to flaunt. Then there are showrooms that deal with imported furniture, meant for opulent and trend-chasing customers. Now, the trendy fibre-blended furniture that lasts long are in the market, and in all probability, it will end up as a rival for the wooden counterparts. Every showroom, normally, will have a workshop, where various designs and patterns are given shape and life by skilled craftsmen. Bosses who have more showrooms will have equally good number of workshops and craftsmen! And the presence of these plush, huge, slightly quaint and luxurious showrooms indicates the potential for employment-generation.

Paint and Marble World Too is Luxurious!

Huge and plush showrooms that deal with hardware and paint- sometimes only paint- and sprawling stockyards with slabs of marble, granite, etc., stacked up are also inextricably linked with construction and real estate sector, that too in prolific way. Chances of indirect employment in the form of painters and craftsmen skilled in decoration work are huge, considering the number of spacious and palatial houses (some owners are crazy enough to erect homes of 7,000 square feet and 12,000 square feet, incredible it may seem, but this is a truth), posh and fabulous malls, supermarkets and hypermarkets that come up across the whole state.

Other sectors: There are big big leather marts, bakeries, stationery shops, huge number of supermarkets and hypermarkets that display every saleable commodity on their racks – even Ayurvedic soaps, shampoos, face-packs, hair oils arrive and fly off the shelves within no time-then automobile spare-parts outlets, middle-of-the-road hotels and restaurants, lined on the left and right of every highway, computer hardware service centres, mobile galleries, mobile shops and service centres, etc. As these types of outlets branch out and provide employment in hundreds and thousands, who can deny the right of trade to be called an industry!

I am not interested in elaborating on further more sectors that do roaring business and provide employment in large numbers. The aforesaid examples are ample proofs for the potential of trade in terms of employment.

Hidden Entrepreneurship or Enterprise!

Up to this point of discussion or debate, we have seen how enterprising businessmen or entrepreneurs, deviating from the trodden path of traditionalism, have emerged successful in their business endeavour to the extent of even matching the calibre of manufacturing bosses. Now, my focus here is on, though small in fiscal strength, 'fledgling or budding' businessmen, who have the potential to transform 'nothingness into somethingness' by way of their hidden or yet-to-blossom entrepreneurship. I do not call them entrepreneurs, but an entrepreneur is in the making in these aspiring souls.

I know a man of thirty years of age, who, I think, is gifted with the 'nose' for business as journalists in media organisations have nose for news. It was on January 30 in 2002, when my mother expired. Funerary rituals were going on when I noticed this man with a kettle of tea and some glasses leaning on the cemetery wall. I was surprised, because in my young days, I have never noticed such an unusual sight of a hotel-owner, waiting for the funeral to end so that he can serve tea for attendees. Death is such a solemn occasion that nobody usually dares to carry out a business and rake in some money since such an attempt will entail nothing but shocking accusations, which may include even the sobriquet or nickname 'corpse-eater.' Because, he is giving vent to his business acumen during a funeral period! Whatever may be the reactions, there is an entrepreneur or enterprising businessman in him waiting to blossom (the best bet for him would have been catering business), because he is 'encashing on a culinary desire, that is always dormant due to unavailability from solemnity of the occasion.'

Normally, funeral takes place in the evening, a convenient time for us Indians to enjoy one or two cups of tea.

I know another guy, who started his career as a tea-server in a hotel at the age of 15 or 16 and went on to become the owner of three hotels by the time he reached the fortieth year of his life. I am so sorry to say that I am tempted to call him an entrepreneur or enterprising businessman because he may have started learning the basics of business from day one and put in all acumen, ability, self-confidence, self-belief, ambition, new strategies and methods, etc., to reach this far!

Now, I am going to talk about a cable channel cum Internet operator, who, in my opinion, is an expert in earning goodwill of his customers. And in the process, he gets more than enough customers and business too! I was able to get Internet connection only through him and surprisingly, he remits my monthly subscription fees and gives me the bill for me to make the payment. At that time, I was his new customer. Once I asked him, "Why you are doing like this, even to new subscribers like me?" Pat came the reply: "All this are being done for long-term gains, you cannot dream of short-term gains here." That's his philosophy of business. He trusts his customers and they in turn cooperate with him. If there is any problem with the connection, he is quick to solve that. He has a vast customer base and it goes on increasing.

Is this not, at least, a spark of entrepreneurship?

I can put forward numerous examples of entrepreneurship or enterprising businessmen from various sectors. Most prominent among them is in food processing, wherein even home-made snacks, including wafers of various types, have a pride of place now. The ingredients for many a snack like rice or wheat or besan powder of different qualities are now brought out by these units. Since paddy cultivation has lost its prominence long back, varieties of boiled rice, consumed only in Kerala, are processed here. Even traditional snacks-usually, they are prepared at home, according to the needs of related season, festival or feast- are processed here and available at bakeries, supermarkets, hypermarkets, etc.. Budding and yet-to-blossom entrepreneurs or enterprising businessmen completely transform 'nothingness into somethingness or even everythingness' through rice or wheat powder, wafers, home-made snacks, pickles of immense varieties- both vegetarian and non-vegetarian like fish, chicken, mutton, beef, etc.- and even spices like chilly, coriander, tamarind, etc., in the form of powder.

At one time, that is about 30 or 40 years back, all these ingredients and end-products were within the four walls of kitchens and the endless imaginative realms of our mothers, sisters and sisters-in-law!

No Wrong Guessing Please!

By this time the reader may have risked a guess. He may have formed an ideal image about an entrepreneur or enterprising businessman as someone who is so scrupulous and uncompromising in his principles and ideals.

Forgot the shocking 2G scam, coal scam, Radia tapes and all such shady deals? The so-called big entrepreneurs were the brains behind them!

Of course, I concur or agree with Victor Hugo, who has said, "Ideal or the most perfect should be the model." In a nation, where law-makers and law-guards are soaked in corruption, I think, complete eradication of that menace is a Utopian concept. As great Kannada writer Dr Sivarama Karanth once said, "The day we achieved independence, we became corrupt."

As far as myself is concerned, ideals are good for oration and not for practice. Prophets and Gods may vow by their ability to take you to heavenly bliss, but the fact of the matter that had happened, is happening and will ever be happening in this mortal world is that those who have pursued ideals with scrupulous precision have bit the dust, been the target of insult, abuse, murderous attacks and even merciless character-assassination. When Mahatma Gandhi was assassinated, the great Irish playwright Bernard Shaw said, "It is not good to be too good." He is right, Gandhi was too good a soul! Then one can imagine what would have been the case If Christ was alive in this age! How could we have a privilege that these masterminds could not?

They are Not Saints!

All said and done, I don't believe that anybody has the objective of social commitment or social obligation or people's welfare as some hacks vouch for entrepreneurs or enterprising businessmen. If that is going to be the case, the world will be the luckiest and Saint Thomas Moore's Utopia will be transformed into a reality. Here too the mantra is 'customer is king' and all, including enterprising businessmen or entrepreneurs, have set their eyes on his pocket.

So naturally, an entrepreneur or an enterprising businessman will adopt several dirty tricks like a traditional businessman. He will follow suit on some survival-tactics like taking care to ensure that his employees are not pampered and his survival is not in jeopardy, then holding his stock (read hoarding) and jacking up the price, when the supply is slack and the demand is high thus placing the customer in a tight spot, fudging accounts by utilizing the services of Chartered Accountants to evade taxes, purchasing and selling goods through illegal routes in order to increase the margin of his profits, etc… Some of them will even violate the border of ethics.

Anyway, sometimes 'small' wrongs may help in realising 'big' rights! Is it not?

So What, that is Natural!

Not a big deal! An entrepreneur or an enterprising businessman is like a tiny tot. He is fresh with new ideas to the world of business as a tiny tot to the world. As babies keep on tottering midway while trying to walk, entrepreneurs too fumble midway while trying to get a foothold in the market, because, in an established scenario, ideas do not get easily stuck. Initially, these ideas will invite only stringent criticism and even become the butt of ridicule of self-styled business masters. The only difference is that the baby will have his/her mummy, daddy or any kith and kin to monitor his/her movements and provide support lest he/she falls and injures himself/herself.

He does not borrow ideas, blessings or any useful tips from his predecessors and charts out his own course. Then it is small wonder that to err is human, but at the same time to rectify-to be absolutely correct- to try not to repeat that error, is also human. After all, experience is the greatest master and he has to learn from his and others' experience, besides his and others' mistakes.

If the novice gets scared and scurries away, he is the loser. No market in the world of business will embrace fresh ideas and ventures with all its heart, soul and stretched-out arms.

So it would be the best if he does not panic or demoralize. He should always believe in the old saying, 'Try, try again, at last you will win.' Pursue with those ideas if the entrepreneur is dead sure about their practicability and potential to provide handsome returns. Try out all options, ways and means to materialize those ideas. At the end of the day, they will bear fruit much to his delight.

PART-II

Preface

Maybe, I am inviting trouble by digging deep into a row, for which many an expert has already 'foisted' their immutable solution on the nation. And a meek and mild media has already lapped it up without a whimper of criticism. Can 'corporate' bias be behind this tail-wagging by media, already debilitated by HMV syndrome? (Every Indian journalist is His Master's Voice (HMV), because proprietor is the editor now. Real editor proposes, but He disposes.)

There is no question of surrendering to the blind assertion that overall development goes neck and neck or hand in hand with economic development. Then how come that so-called economically developed states like Maharashtra limp behind states like Kerala in social as well as human resource development and consequently physical quality of life, standard of living and many other development indicators!

I am neither an economist nor an expert in economics, evolved from my experiences in print media. But practical results are just in contradiction with theoretical assumptions. What has gone wrong or where has it happened?

Here too, I am tempted to compare the process called development to a coin with heads and tails, wherein both are not at all the same. Heads stands for quantitative development and tails represents quantitative cum qualitative development. Where should Maharashtra and Kerala stand?

Maybe, reality is too bitter a pill to swallow!!!

The Author

Relook at Development is Necessary!

Why there was the need for a debate on industry, the reader may wonder! The necessity of a discussion on the process called industry cropped up from the experts' bias against certain states, whose Human Development Index and Social Development Index are far higher than others, including those with a high Economic Development Index. Solely because, I think, experts are adamant that unless and until there is a vibrant and lively manufacturing or production sector, no state can flaunt itself as industrially developed or economically developed. Strange!

I think it is wrong to conclude that overall development is directly proportional to economic development. In our country itself, there are states with high economic development indicators. Surprisingly, their performance with regard to social as well as human resource development is poor.

I think economic development is only a means to overall development. A nation can claim the status of overall development only when it has high social development indicators in consequence of high human resource development indicators. I feel sans any equally high economic development indicators, no nation or state can realise the so-called overall development.

Kerala is the Case in Point!

Take the case of one of the most 'enterprising' states in this country, Kerala, where there is nothing to be excited about, production-wise or manufacturing-wise (the state has very less number of manufacturing and production units). But it has a flourishing health sector, a thriving education sector, a booming hospitality sector besides a robust construction sector. Banking is another zone that deserves a special mention with its brilliant performance, quite evident from the fact that Kerala has a very high savings density. Now, *avatar* of the most modern development or digital development that can 'electronicise' or computerize functions or operations with minimum number of human capital by means of its software mantra-Information Technology-is spreading its wings and may fly into unimaginable heights by utilizing the state's highly efficient and intelligent manpower. Moreover, it is one of the most developing tourist economies in the world, as quoted by one of the leading English magazines.

All these silver linings are not simply an urban phenomenon as in other states or the much-touted economically developed states. The progress has penetrated right into the rural heart. So much so that Kerala is the only state in this country, worthy to be called a city- state in the real sense: a big city, sub-divided into corporation cities, municipality towns, A-grade village towns, B-grade village towns and C-grade village towns with a posh and rich look, skilled and highly paid human capital and a friendly atmosphere. Friendly atmosphere does not indicate an abject humility before employers.

Exceptions, anomalies, shortages and all sorts of negative aspects are there, only to the extent of being in a reasonable minority. But experts, intelligentsia and even the common public in the state exaggerate the situation to an unlimited proportion. This is because complacency, smugness and even jingoism have no place here.

There are enough doomsayers here because nobody buys their minimum-wages-maximum-benefit agenda. At the same time, employers should not be bled white due to impudence of their workforce. The 'Lal Salam' influence had, has and will be having its impact, but there are counter-forces too to nullify that. After all, nature stipulates that every action should have an opposite and equal reaction.

Whether we like it or not, as long as poverty exists in this world there will be Communism too, at least in a modified form.

Where is fair Distribution of Development in Maharashtra?

For last many years, I have come across the hollow talk of decentralization of power, authority, policies, etc.. Not even a faint cry for decentralization of development or fairly distributive development. I am talking about decentralization of development or fair distribution of development at provincial or state level. In other terms, we need an urban-rural equality and not an urban-rural disparity. Let us leaf through the pages of one of the most industrially developed states in the country Maharashtra with high economic indicators. It basks in the glory of financial capital of the country Mumbai, where hundreds, thousands and even millions flock to grab an opportunity so that they can climb up the ladder of life and place themselves on the topmost rung, where hundreds of traders, dealing with everything under the sun, pay a compulsory visit as it is a great source for their raw materials and a potential market for their produce, where almost all companies set up their office to facilitate and establish an international link and where so many multi-national companies (MNCs) have a huge presence in all kinds of industries, even the ignored ones that wait for an emphatic approval of experts.

See the Vertical Development!

But what about the physical quality of life or PQL in this megapolis! Dismally poor! Here I recall the comment of a friend on his visit to Kerala: "I do not find any vertical development in the state."

Of course, you can gape at more skyscrapers and hypermarkets in Mumbai. Luxurious and plush malls, that can stun you with their dazzling splendour, outnumber all other cities in the country. Why not? It has a population count on its way to 2 crore. Anyway, India's best, swankiest and the most fabulous or magnificent mall is in Kochi-Lulu Mall − and the Queen of Arabian Sea has only an aggregate population of 30 lakh, including the floating one. Unfortunately, according to a survey, 60 percent of Mumbai malls are registering very low footfall.

Here comes the oxymoronic situation that one can perceive in this most populated metropolis. Sixty percent of its inmates smilingly curse away their life in slums, made of scrap iron for the wretched lot or cement and bricks for the just 'privileged' few among them, and constricted to the most minimal level. I won't reduce them to the situation, depicted by John Keats in his Ode to Nightingale, "Where men sit and groan." Rather I would like to say, "Where men squat, smile and lavish away their life with all amenities like refrigerator, television, radio, computer, laptop, scooter, motorbike and even car, Metro, monorail, local electric trains etc., in and around respectively." That too in an area of maximum 200 square feet with common toilets, always squalid and congested. In what can be termed as the greatest example of Mumbaikars' extra-ordinary skill in adaptability, it is heard that one such filthy and nauseating toilet is shared by 15 families. Notwithstanding, they do not blame it on anybody because of the unrealistic prospect of earning minimum Rs 20 lakh if the property is sold. That is a hypothetic situation. When they can accommodate with such a narrow space with its unimaginable restrictions and constrictions, what problem they will face with financial, geographical, climatic, social, communal or any such catastrophes that Mumbai is habituated to. It is heard that even if the government or any charity organization, in a philanthropic gesture, hands them over the keys of a better and more spacious abode, they prefer to sell it at the huge market rates rather than shift.

Like a leech which can never stay in a snug or cosy bed with all the ingredients that impart warm comfort. By all means, it will crawl back into its favourite haunt: the muddy earth soaked in filth, dirt and weeds! You just do not have a solution for such a situation!

Something to be Greatly Proud of?

I have heard Mumbaikars priding themselves in the much-talked-about aphorism: "if you survive in Mumbai, you can survive anywhere." They are absolutely right. Only a Mumbaikar can squat and relieve himself so unabashedly and unshamefacedly, that too in the open, and clean his ass with a 750 ml bottle of water! Just have a 'breezy' jaunt in

Mumbai's jam-packed electric locals and 'enjoy' the stinking odour, wafting from the peripheries or outer limits of railway tracks! Agreed! None in other cities can even dream of such a ludicrous situation because they do not have such 'high economic indicators'! Not only that, Mumbaikars are experts in converting helplessness into greatness as politicians are adept in making virtue out of vice.

So much for my friend's 'vertical' development!

Now, let us peep through the condition of privileged flat inmates. Surely, they are better placed as they move around in a 400 to 450 square feet, 650 to 750 square feet or at the most 1,000 square feet area. All structures above that limit are elevated to a higher status in accordance with the importance and reputation of the area by the names 3-BHK, 4-BHK, etc., flats. The latest statistics has endowed these flat-owners with land-ownership too as they possess 400 to 450 square feet, 650 to 750 square feet, 1,000 square feet, etc., of land! Maybe, this is the smallest land ownership ever recorded. Anyway, something is better than nothing!

Joint Families in Such a Narrow Space!

According to the latest trend, these 3-BHKs, 4-BHKs, etc., are now being converted into joint families. More simply put, three brothers of a family in a joint venture and with an equal share buy a 3-BHK flat and possess one bedroom each to accommodate their respective family; the hall is common for all. We have no choice left except to astound at the sense of space that Mumbaikars have developed in recent times. Not surprising, considering their ability in managing space by accommodating more people in too narrow rooms. This writer had the 'privilege' to share a single room, hardly of

200 square feet area, with three more people at a daily rent of Rs 200 per bed in a lodge. Fortunately, the lodge-owner would always ensure that the toilets are clean and well-maintained. Renting out a 1-BHK or 2-BHK at the rate of Rs 25,000 per month, of course, to be shared by 3 people and on the 24th floor, would have strained my coffers (this was the rate prevalent in Andheri in 2013). Incredible, in view of the fact that I was born, brought up and spoiled in a very spacious house in the 'industrially backward' Kerala. Luckily, I haven't developed the habit of 'priding myself' like the most tolerant, resilient and even thick-skinned Mumbaikars!

If enterprising businessmen are entrepreneurs, these Mumbaikars are 'spacepreneurs,' considering the novel methods they make use of in managing the already mismanaged space situation in the maximum city, which ruling eagles of Maharashtra aspire to transfigure into a world class city! I wish all the success in their Himalayan task. Easily said than done, when one takes into consideration the all-round abysmal depth into which the city has fallen.

Travelling blues: The travelling woes or blues, another black mark of the most populated metropolitan city in the country, pathetically reflect on the quality of life it can afford. Lucky are those who travel by BEST buses or other four-wheelers-not so fortunate because of the traffic snarl-ups and jams due to road repairs and constructions-when compared to the hapless souls, who rely on suburban train service. The average footfall per day is 75 lakh here. In fact, these commuters do not board, they virtually squeeze into these coaches and squeeze out at their destination. You need not squeeze out, just place yourself at the doorstep of the compartment, your co-commuters will ensure that you are out on the platform. Same is the situation in the case of entry. So mechanical are the entry and exit. And inside the compartment, that 15 or 30 or 60 minutes of travel is like a tiresome task inside a jam-packed room. You feel extremely exhausted once you finish it. Actually, one has to relax and travel, in Mumbai, especially in suburban trains, you sweat and travel!

I condemn such type of high economic development that cannot ensure high quality of life, as a farce, foisted upon a 'gullible' people who think too much of themselves, by way of myopic strategies and policies!

What about other cities like Pune, Nagpur, Nashik, Aurangabad, etc., in the state? Most of them are lesser evils except Pune that is catching up with Mumbai and will hopefully become a Mumbai sooner than later. The ruling eagles are happy over it as that possibility backs up their efforts to transform these corporations into metropolitan cities.

These short-sighted efforts will end up in only urbanization at the cost of rural Maharashtra. It has already happened and nobody seems to have noticed or is it that they want to project the particular phase as a prelude to a greater development in the making due to liberalization policies, as figured out and promised by many of our computer-brained intellectuals in the media. As a great English essayist-maybe Bertrand Russell- points out, *'What guarantee is there certain losses will be compensated by some uncertain gains'*!

The gains are nowhere in sight. Even the country's percentage of growth is going down despite the efforts by fiscal managers to arrest that trend. The prediction of economic surveys keeps on fluctuating and does not promise any steady growth.

Experiences oblige me to thunder at the thoughtless liberalization policies that have gnawed into the core of our economy, as increasingly clear from the low quality of life that hundreds, thousands and even millions in this country poignantly, and some like Mumbaikars with pride, take in their stride. The economic recession that the country and the world have been pushed into during last several years and whose ghost is still lurking about, is another reminder.

Liberalisation policies have only liberalised all market, civic, administrative, bureaucratic and governmental forces, already at their venomous best by virtue of the moral degradation that this country and the world have undergone. Even the government has let go of the rein and reduced itself to the status of a mute spectator, then one can imagine the likely chaotic scenario. The employers are pampered under the pretext of attracting more investments. Employees are always at the receiving end and demoralised by the resultant loss in their privileges. Unless a system, that can take both these groups hand in hand, comes into being, I think, this friction in some states or meek surrender in some others will continue. How long this meek surrender? Let us hope, this suppression may not breed frustration followed by unrest, today or tomorrow!

My humble knowledge in economics, derived from practical observations and experiences and not by mugging up millions of idiocies that throng the media, teaches me that this country begs for a mixed economy. In a march past there is always left, right, left right and so on............ This is quite visible in every sphere of life. Likewise, in every forward march, including the economic march, there has to be right (liberalization) and then left (protectionism) and so forth, according to the need! It can never be right, right, right, right........... as the rightist fundamentalist among intellectuals will prefer nor it can be left, left, left, left............... as leftist fundamentalists will aspire.

Housing rates differ from those of Mumbai in proportion with the value of money in the respective cities. Here too nobody is carping at anybody or anything because of the unrealistic prospect of earning a huge sum, when the property is sold. These souls too have the same tolerance level as Mumbaikars. To drive home my point, I have heard a Nagpurian lamenting, "When will Nagpur transform into a Mumbai, God"? Poor soul! He wants the reasonably good quality of life in Nagpur to downgrade into an abject level like in Mumbai!

Mumbai's Contribution to GDP is 60 Percent

From the reality that Mumbai contributes more than 60 percent to the GDP (gross domestic product or the total value of all the goods and services produced by a state) of Maharashtra, one can infer the kind of development the rural parts have undergone (I think 60 percent is my guess and generosity, actually the figure may be bigger). The state has about 12 plus crore in its population kitty and Mumbai about 1.80 crore. This proves that 1.80 crore Mumbaikars contribute 60 percent to the state's GDP. The remaining 40 percent is contributed by rest of the population 10 crore.

The yawning gulf between Mumbai and the rest of Maharashtra can be made out from this data itself. Not for nothing that a survey in the 2000s, monitored by the Union Government, showed that 11 in the state come under the category of 100 most backward districts in the country, most of them in Vidarbha region.

Here, in these 11 districts, the degree of backwardness is the highest. That means there are a good number of districts of varying backwardness in the state. To have a correct image, just go on a pleasure trip through the Vidarbha region. This writer had seen with his own eyes the kind of backwardness that the region had been subjected to, or maybe, is experiencing, on his way from Nagpur to Pune. In some places, you can gape at thatched roofs, sometimes huts of scrap iron or houses like shop rooms, of course, made of cement and bricks. Another worrying survey indicates that 50 percent of Maharashtra population live in slums or houses of very poor quality and bad condition.

How Mumbai Pools in so much for GDP!

Why Mumbai pools in so much for GDP? Because it has more resources than the rest of Maharashtra-a difference which can be compared to that between an elephant and a rat. How? Because it has more in-built and later additions in the name of infrastructure and for the same reason it used to draw human capital from all over the country in hundreds, thousands and even millions and wealthy entrepreneurs or investors from within and abroad. As is the norm in our society, member with the highest income in a family will have a dominating hand and impact. Mumbai had that advantage and it capitalized on the resultant situation. It is ridiculous, but I have no alternative except to mention that- if media reports are factual- leaders from Western Maharashtra (abode of the aggressive sugar lobby in the state) normally divert funds, earmarked for Vidarbha, to their areas. Can Mumbai leaders lag behind? Then what is wrong in the continuing hue and cry for a separate state of Vidarbha! Can anybody stand such kind of brazen neglect!

Its leaders fortified the Mumbai castle to the maximum by grabbing major chunk of funds from the state coffers, nudging out other backward regions like Vidarbha and Marathwada , enhancing all kinds of infrastructure and generating opportunities of all hues, so much so that it ended up in so low a quality of life. Its leaders are still bragging of the material advantages, when the so-called advantages are there for everybody to see.

How? There were too many takers or stakeholders for spoils (amenities, facilities, utilities, conveniences, etc.,) that this huge industrial mammoth created. Suppose it had enough spoils for hundreds, takers were in thousands and even millions. The demand was uncontrollably huge and supply in shortage in an equal measure. That mismatch ended up in skyrocketing prices of land, buildings, flats, apartments, etc., and consequently led to the most unequal or unjust situation, wherein even 5 percent of Mumbai population cannot afford a qualitative life! Even today there is no change in that trend. If you have more money, you can earn more and enjoy life more in Mumbai. Nothing will create nothing here because all currents and trends are against such hapless people. Even the government will not come to their rescue.

In my opinion, minimum 70 percent of the population should be able to enjoy a reasonably good quality of life, if not high or excellent, provided they believe in the principle, 'be more productive and earn more.' Otherwise, what is the fun in development and progress!

Chaos Personified!

It is better to forget about the chaotic situation and the tragedies which follow this impulsive rat race that Mumbai has been witnessing. On one side, Illegal structures, erected by throwing all the norms to wind, are coming up like mushrooms and on the other, so many of them are collapsing like playing cards. Builders in collusion with bureaucrats and people's representatives are on a construction spree. In between many such structures crumble and cave in resulting in the loss of large number of lives. This is not all. The simultaneous erection and collapse is spreading out beyond the city limits, say for example, to Mumbra, Thane etc.. The demolition of illegal structures, erected under the blessing hands of civic officials and people's representatives, is another tragedy. Then full-throated weeping and lamenting, breast-beating and all sorts of histrionics follow! Why to talk or discuss much! The financial capital is always replete with cries, protests and agitations thereafter and poor Mumbaikars, besides their own, bear up this burden too.

And the most alarming of all, as hygiene, sanitation, pollution (credit goes to manufacturing or production giants, who never bother to ensure the stipulated safeguards) and other health-related factors are so disgraceful that Mumbai is increasingly becoming the favourite hub for all kinds of epidemics in the world. Whenever any corner of the world starts sneezing, Mumbai catches flu! If any new diseases are invented, (pharmaceutical companies in the West have no other assignments than creating new diseases and rolling out required drugs) Mumbai becomes its breeding ground in India. It is now susceptible to all kinds of flu like swine flu, bird flu today, maybe, turkey flu, cow flu, buffalo flu tomorrow, who knows what else! The shocking reports of sewage water mixing up with drinking water in the city limits are outrageous. Which hell is now going to break loose! God alone knows!

If heavy rains, storm, cyclone and all weather-related devils pound or bombard with all fury, the financial capital caves in and submerges in their watery and windy might. Then the most hellish sufferings, misery, pain, etc., are 'unleashed' and you will find all citizens, irrespective of caste, creed, religion, profession, etc., reeling and writhing under the terrible impact. Not a big deal since most of the city areas do not even boast of drainage system worth its spelling, as every inch has been allotted to real estate sharks for converting into flats and apartments worth millions and billions.

Just imagine the situation when summer is at its scorching worst and drought-like monster is stalking the whole state, especially those impoverished and backward districts!

You will find every Mumbaikar in all 'unprivileged' areas running hither and thither and scampering after drinking water-tankers for buckets of water to quench his thirst and hunger. Ground water level might have reached its nadir or the lowest point long back, because millions and millions have 'screwed' and are still 'screwing' the city for a 'dreamcometrue.'

And you will come across reports and photographs, splashed across the whole length and breadth of Indian media, both electronic and print, of pauperised and famished souls from Latur and other drought-ridden districts, 'huddled together like criminals in rags' or 'heaped like garbage here and there' in various corners of Mumbai suburbs. Perhaps, they are waiting for 'the manna from the heaven called Mantralaya.'

The magnificent and lusty green cover, Mumbai used to be proud of, has been torn into pieces and shreds for skyscrapers and colossal buildings that stand tall and up to the vagaries of Nature and its five elements. How long? A slight jerk due to the tectonic imbalance is sufficient to tremble and topple these huge and concrete structures. Can the mighty Earth in the country's financial capital withstand the huge gravitational force these monstrous structures that proliferate like ants impose on it?

In short, Mumbaikar will be well warned against a sword of Damocles, always hanging over his head and the impending disaster, in the form of tremor or flood or drought, etc., can be at any moment!

My goodness! This is the quality life that liberalization policies are promising us! I think the country is paying a heavy price for leaving these market, civic, administrative, bureaucratic, governmental and all other powerful and evil forces to their whims and fancies. The government, on its part, should play a regulatory role even in a federal set-up!

Our first Prime Minister Jawaharlal Nehru, mesmerized by its picturesque beauty in the 50s, had extolled Kashmir like this: if there is a heaven on Earth, it is this, it is this, it is this!

May I pity Mumbai like this: if there is a hell in India, it is this, it is this, it is this?

The Senseless Media Hype!

Then what was this hype, hoopla, ruckus etc., about Mumbai and Maharashtra in the 80s and 90s! That was the creation of media. Just turn your memory clock back and try to recall the senseless media hype when Chandrababu Naidu was Chief Minister of old Andhra Pradesh! The media turned the whole country upside down in its attempt to convince whole of us how his policies were going to transform his state and everything in this country into gold, just like the philosopher's stone of the Alchemists! I still remember how those snobs (I mean those in the media who drool at the mention of the United States of America and Western countries!) were eagerly looking forward to the visit of Bill Clinton to Andhra Pradesh and Chandrababu Naidu's reaction, as if his response was going to 'unleash' a shower of gold into the country in the form of foreign investments! Next General Elections followed by Assembly Elections saw Chandrababu Naidu and his TDP vanishing into thin air because of the merciless drubbing. Within no time, media forgot about his poster-boy status and dumped Naidu by the roadside forever. When he was gone, the condition of Andhra Pradesh became crystal clear as truth and realities opened up themselves for everybody to see. Now, he has become the Chief Minister of new Andhra Pradesh and we can wait for another thoughtless hype!

Then Ramalinga Raju, another poster boy and symbol of India's future industrial glory, again as made out by our media. Just imagine, for about 25 years with his flagship project, Satyam Computers, this man took the country for a stupefying ride and hoodwinked us, minting millions and billions in the process. Even then the media could not sniff out the diabolic intention of feathering his nest at the cost naïve citizens. In the end, thanks to this 'great' entrepreneur, he had the guts and spine to speak his heart out and revealed how he had been looting this 'great nation with great culture and tradition' for so many years, much to the bewilderment of the hare-brained media with a very low sense of reality and intelligently idiotic enough to make sweeping and impulsive judgements or assessments.

We can expect the same travesty in the case of Narendra Modi. Gujarat was hyped up and propped up to such an alarming proportion that Narendra Modi has now been pitchforked to the central corridors of power and he is waving his 'Make in India' wand no end! Now, everybody in the country, especially the rightist fundamentalists in the media (like Mulla Mulayam who was branded as secular fundamentalist for his pathological affinity towards Muslim minoritysm), is looking forward to the pearls of wisdom likely to fall from our gregarious Prime Minister's saffron mouth! There will be no match for Gujarat and many self-styled experts will eulogise the Gujarat model for others to emulate! No matter its social development indicators are on an average scale and human development index is glaringly poor! And a time may come when Modi may meet the same 'Naidu fate' as his voters, on a dark day, may slam their doors on him. Then he will be swept aside and whirled into the quicksand of oblivion by the same media which glorified him! That situation may mark an eye-opener for one and all, including Gujarathis, his fans in the media, critics, rivals etc..

Investment hype! The investment hype is another fallacy or mistaken belief! The moment many MoUs (memoranda of understanding) are signed, the media get carried away and start speculating like the woman with a basket of eggs on her head. I have always made out that if MoUs for an investment of 1 lakh crore are inked (which means there are investment proposals worth Rs 1 lakh crore), only 25 percent of that total worth become a reality. If further clarified, only investments amounting to Rs 25,000 crore materialize and it may take even five and more years. Long before that these hacks with their tails up start counting the unhatched chickens. An abrupt or an unexpected turn of events in global economic arena will suffice to topple that basket of eggs. Most of the time, the proposals fizzle out like the smashed eggs due to uncertainty in ruling circles or any other fiscal fiasco.

I remember one of my colleagues in print media asserting that Chhattisgarh was the most developing state in the country 10 years back, because it had attracted investments worth Rs 1 to 2 lakh crore. I was surprised because I had spent four years of my life in Raipur, the capital of Chhattisgarh and arguably the most clogged, crammed, even congested and the dirtiest city in the country, solely due to the ubiquitous presence of shabby cycle-rickshaws and shitty odour from all around. Not only that, these crawling three-wheeled cycles may bring not only traffic but also the whole life of that city into a squeezing halt. So immense is their reach and hold in the city under the benign grace of a people's representative, who, at any cost, will ensure its perennial presence. That sight itself is reflective of the development that Chhattisgarh might have witnessed. Then it has a festering wound in the form of Bastar, where Naxalites are playing Robinhoods!

So much for the media's mindless hype over any economic development!

Why and how this Happened?

Why this has happened, is still happening and will be happening for years to come in Mumbai and rest of Maharashtra? To be honest, this will happen and keep on happening unless the ruling eagles effect a shift in their crucial policies, stop efforts with the objective of creating metropolitan cities, and nurture all districts, including municipalities and panchayats, so that they can stand on their feet and develop. They will be well advised to accept that human resource is the greatest of all resources of a nation or a state and development of each and every one of them is of utmost importance for the overall progress of a nation or a state; that economic development of a nation or a state cannot be achieved without an equally vibrant rural economy.

Rampant urbanization: Nothing inhibits me from declaring that the first culprit is the rampant urbanization at the cost of rural Maharashtra! Urbanisation, if it is transformation of rural areas into posh municipal towns or village towns with all facilities that an urban centre can boast of, well and good, but if it is the consequence of mindless exodus of people from panchayats or villages and municipalities to district headquarters and big cities, then I look upon it with the sheer contempt it merits. This is what has happened In Maharashtra. For the same reason, the state has only pockets of development adjoining the municipal corporations, big cities or perchance some district headquarters, Mumbai pocket being the largest and the mightiest! And they too are undergoing the same transformation that the financial capital of the country had, because of an exceedingly high density of population: an economic development with high indicators but very poor quality of life.

Poor panchayats! I don't think there is any village or panchayat in the state that can claim to have a population of 5,000. Then what development you can expect from these small pockets with such a very low density of population! Even if Panchayati Raj is strengthened and activated to its fullest potential, can these people be lured back into their land of birth and everything that followed! Then what are the governments and its authorities are going to do to improve this pathetic situation? The concerned authorities will be well requested to stop these efforts to create metropolitan cities and go for division of the state into at least two or three parts for easier administration, complete decentralization of power or stronger Panchayati Raj system and better allocation of funds. High-pitched grandstanding and no practice will yield only 'nothing.'

Rural areas ignored! In the no-holds-barred industrialization that Maharashtra launched in 60s, 70s, and 80s and is continuing even today, its governments simply brushed aside and are still brushing aside the rural sector and its traditional and indigenous resource agriculture. Now, the state is not famous for its agricultural output, but notorious for the suicides of farmers that has caught international attention. The state governments, one after the other, projected industry as the greatest and the most lucrative resource and failed to sow its seeds in rural parts under the pretext of poor infrastructure!

Where does the infrastructure come from? Does it fall from the skies and heavens above or gush out from bowels of the earth? It was and is and will always be the duty of the governments, central and state, to erect or construct or build roads that connect and interconnect cities, towns and villages, flyovers, lanes, streets, all structures, enclosures and everything which constitute infrastructure.

Do not degrade ourselves to think that only urbanites are entitled to a cosy and comfortable life!

Undue promotion: Yet another folly was the chauvinistic promotion of Mumbai as the ultimate destination instead of Maharashtra through a high-pitched media blitz, both print and TV, and the indiscriminate dumping of funds in the financial capital with the least regard for remaining districts and regions. So what? This ended up in an uncontrollable migration to the state, chiefly and incomparably Mumbai, from all over the country and even the rest of Maharashtra, again mainly and incomparably- earlier from 50s onwards from South of the country and now from the North. The South already has its own ultimate destinations, and maybe with an eye to accommodate its local human capital, is going for only a mellowed campaign. This culminated in a 'curse in disguise' to Mumbai, which attracted migrants in hundreds and thousands. Even now the trend continues although with, maybe, less intensity.

Education Can Make the Difference!

How is development of each and every one of the human resources possible? A conventional reply can be, through literacy, but that luxury will only enable him to know what he can achieve. But knowledge is an indispensible necessity and nothing less than power. However, it can be attained only through education, not the simple education, but the quality education by which the recipient can compete with anyone from any part of the country! Why? Because that stimulates his ambition. Ambition will strengthen his self-belief, then he can be aware of his rights as a citizen of the country and the state apart from the possibilities required for self-development. More than enough for his and the state's development! And quality should be measured only by the standard of teaching! There shouldn't be any compromise on that aspect!

In short, education can be defined as a process that can make you aware of your own good qualities, bad qualities, strengths, weakness etc., consequently your own potential. For that there is no need that you should enrol in any of the aforesaid schools, colleges, institutions, institutes etc.. Because, if to quote Socrates, the great Greek philosopher, 'Knowledge of thyself is the greatest knowledge.' Which means awareness of one's own potential is the greatest necessity. One need not be part of any institutions; even ordinary artisans, skilled workers, porters, building painters, masons, carpenters, daily-wagers, servants, etc., can achieve this possibility by just keeping his eyes, ears and mind open for absorbing the inherent knowledge in and around by seeing, hearing and through experience. No master is superior to experience! Only an individual can materialize it with his unrelenting efforts, self-esteem and consequent self-belief!

More importantly and essentially, education should enable us to think with our head instead of our heart! It should make us aware of our rights as human beings, our rights as citizens of the state and the country. It should also enlighten us with the truth that all facilities, amenities and comforts that constitute the process called development are our fundamental right and not the generosity of our representatives in Assembly, Parliament or civic bodies like municipality and panchayat! Otherwise, education is worth a rubbish package!

How is the quality? Is the quality of education in Maharashtra satisfying? From the very truth that came to light some 10 or more years back, my suspicious fingers are surely directed towards that anomaly. The man on the executive seat of a distinguished university was churning out degree documents at Rs 15,000 (sorry, if the amount mentioned is false; it couldn't be less because he might not have been foolish enough to issue certificates at less than that rate!) each and it took 15 years for a journalist to smell out the truth and expose.

If any nosy journalist or media person endeavours to excavate deep into the depths of the past, more such dark truths will come out in the open. Maharashtra with its docile psyche and vulnerability to all kinds of political, social and intellectual manipulations, might have played, may be playing and will be playing unsuspectingly host to such dark realities.

Following is an interesting situation that the aforesaid distinguished university had slipped into! I am not sure whether the university has extricated itself from that precarious position by this time! This happened during 2004 to 2006 period and is related to MSW course. There were 60 students majoring in that subject, out of which 30 were from Kerala.

I have heard people in several states boasting how their universities are attracting people from every nook and corner of the country. Nothing of that sort has ever happened nor will ever happen! No university in this country can claim to have every subject in its repertory of courses. In that case, students may move over to the university of their choice in pursuit of the course of their liking.

Here comes the emotional crick or the shock due to self-deceit! In Kerala, at that time, students were supposed to overcome the hurdle of a preliminary examination to get a slot for MSW course. Aside from that, they were supposed to pay Rs 1 lakh as annual fees. In the said university, there was no hiccup such as examination and students were instructed to pay only Rs 20,000 as fees. So, a free-for-all situation for aspiring students, who, normally set their ambition on foreign countries like US, Canada, UK, Australia, New Zealand and those in Europe with a MSW in hand. That was the attraction for these Kerala students, who had aspired to fly abroad.

The jocular part is here! There were 11 or 14 lecturers and only 4 of them were fluent in English, which implies that only 4 of them know to speak and write in English. Rest were fluent mainly in Marathi. Just imagine the predicament of those Kerala students. Anyway, that piquant situation was not an issue for them. Most of them passed the examination with a First Class grade. How did they manage to come out successful? Four of the Kerala students were staying in the same building where I was. One of them, who, I think, is now in Ireland, revealed the secret of their success and I was thunderstruck! Following are his words: 'Sir, a student need not write correct answers, he can scribble anything, any bullshit, even swearwords, only thing is that he should have many sheets in answer paper. The number of sheets counts here, nothing else. You can pass with a First Class grade hands down, no problem!'

Belittling English will ultimately boomerang because that language is our window to the world of wisdom and science. Bang-shutting that window will only cut us and our country off from rest of the world! For what purpose! For our disastrous future only, nothing else!

The Sloppy Delivery System!

Above all these factors, inextricably linked to make development effective or defective, is the most important and the least highlighted delivery system. So sloppy and sleazy is the functioning of this system in this country that no state can claim immunity from this gaping hole, which belches out all attempts at development. How it happens?

Suppose the government has allocated Rs 1,000 crore for various development works in Vidarbha region. It may or may not reach corporations, municipalities and gram panchayats in that region. From that phase itself the delivery system becomes vulnerable to all kinds of manipulations. The efficiency and sincerity of people's representatives of concerned civic bodies matter a lot. Where is sincerity? Then forget about efficiency! Apart from that, the illegal diversion of funds allocated for one region to another due to the impertinent intervention of powerful representatives, whose writ runs more than anybody else's in the corridors of power. The government itself indulges in this malpractice when its coffers become thinner and thinner. Then comes the real situation that mars the delivery system. From civic bodies, the funds allotted for various works or projects do not reach the intended spot and beneficiaries, it gets gobbled up midway, changing hands and green notes among good number of officials, whom we 'lovingly hammer' as bureaucracy, though these are petty bureaucrats. The bigger sharks with IAS, IRS or IFS are inside state secretariats and Central durbar and their meddling is with huge projects and proposals of astronomical worth!

At the end of the situation, hardly 30 percent is spent or expended on execution of the particular project!

In this context, I remember an incident that will strengthen my point on delivery system. When I was in Bhopal, the capital of Madhya Pradesh, during 1993-96 period, daily in the morning, I used to have a tea-cum-discussion in a small shop in that ward, run by a man in his 50s. We used to discuss several topics like politics, development and even the deplorable condition of roads in that ward. Mind you, corporator of the ward resides there and would join our discussion. I am quoting his words: "BMC or Bhopal Municipal Corporation has allotted Rs 5 lakh for road repair works in this ward, but I have never come across any representation or request or protest or agitation by the residents. Obviously you can guess where the fund goes." Which emphasizes that no people's representative will take any initiative on his own accord; that he has to be prodded to do some beneficial deeds for citizens! The political service of this nation has come to such a reckless pass! If there is no initiative from citizens, naturally the money will go to his or her or 'their' coffers!

What will he or she do if his or her fingers get stuck in a jaggery pot? How can he or she straightaway clean those fingers, that too without licking them to his or her fill?

It's the People Who Develop a Nation!

So, now it is quite crystal-clear that it is the people and not the government servants or the so-called politicians who develop a nation.

Because democracy is of the people, by the people and for the people!

Again, it is absurd to take it for granted that you have voted them to power, because we are living in an era, wherein a father will mock at his son for frittering away any golden chance to take bribe!

I feel we should stop evaluating economic development and the consequent overall development in terms of GDP, unless contributions from various regions are uniform. Such a scenario does not arise in the case of Maharashtra, where Mumbai contributes at least 60 percent. If the situation continues going downhill (already, in Mumbai, Kurla-Ghatkopar belt has overtaken Dharavi as the biggest slum area in Asia. Now, only 60 percent of Mumbai population cover the slum area, tomorrow, in a worsening scenario or context, it may go up), then I think there will be nothing wrong in considering the state as the finest example for the figure of speech in English language called oxymoron: Maharashtra is rich, but Maharashtrians are poor just as India is rich, but Indians are poor (there is nothing wrong in the latter statement because as per historical calculations, India was the richest nation in the world till 17th century).

Not only that, today Maharashtra has the highest GDP in the country by virtue of its 12+ crore population, the financial capital Mumbai and an inflationary economy, wherein the value of money goes down and down because of a huge gap between demand and supply or availability, the former being on the rise and the latter on the wane, sure, under the 'malignant grace' of market, civic, administrative, bureaucratic, governmental and all other powerful and evil forces. Tomorrow it may end up as the state with the highest GDD (gross domestic degradation).

And I think value of money is not its purchasing but utility or usefulness value. Suppose 1 BHK flat costs Rs 1 crore in the financial capital of the country (not surprising, in the latest trend, 1 BHK is worth Rs 57 lakh in Thane) and in Nagpur if you can purchase 3 such flats with that amount, the orange city has an edge over Mumbai as the former has a better value of money than the latter. Convincingly, Nagpur should have a better quality of life than in Mumbai. Undoubtedly it is so.

Anyway, perfection can be yearned, craved and at the most strenuously strived for with the objective of attaining. Where is the guarantee for its realization? Then what! Try for a first, second or third rank and get at least a distinction!

Kerala is a Different Cup of Tea, Yaar!

This has not happened, is not happening and I don't think will ever happen in Kerala unless its governments and people squander away the edges gained by way of neutral policies. Why? Firstly, it is the smallest among bigger states like Maharashtra, Tamil Nadu, Karnataka, Madhya Pradesh, Uttar Pradesh etc., with only 14 districts, located within the reach of each other and linked or accessible to each other by way of an intricate network of roads, flyovers, bridges-small and big- transport and communication facilities. Lesser number of districts itself enables a smooth and viable administration.

Almost all anomalies or drawbacks or discrepancies, which make a mockery of the process called development in Mumbai and Maharashtra, exist in this most literate state too, but comparatively in a lesser measure and intensity. Even against these lesser evils, such a vehement hue and cry breaks loose from the side of citizens that authorities will have no alternative except to subdue to their demands. Here people believe that all processes in the form of development are their fundamental right and not the generosity of any of the people's representatives. By way of such stringent and extreme measures only, many proposals have realized, though sometimes they cross the boundary of propriety and legitimacy. As the saying goes, only crying babies get the milk!

Simply wishing and sitting still or at the most sulking, will not win any day for anyone here. Of course, there are docile elements too, who raise their tail and scamper away. Luckily, they are in great minority. Even the middle class or the bourgeoisies, always in the habit of sheepishly taking advantage of the blood, sweat and tears, shed by other classes, are vocal and vibrant here lest they lose their due or rights. Ultimately, as I have said earlier, it is the people who develop a nation, government is only a facilitator.

Gulf Boom in 70s Set the Tone!

No urbanisation here in the style of several other states through rampant migration from rural to urban areas. From here, people migrate to major cities or other states and then abroad like Middle East, Europe, US, Canada, etc.. It was Gulf boom in the 70s that set the tone for the overall turnaround in situation. Even the remotest villages in the state, too distant from the phenomenon called development, were part of this sudden upsurge. The trend was not confined to any particular region of the state like Travancore or Kochi or Malabar. It was a groundswell from every junction across the state, followed by today's fair distribution of development. Hence the rich-looking villages that are the hallmarks and indicators of the kind of development that rural parts have undergone! Within 5 to 10 square miles or square kilometres of a village, you will get all facilities that a city or a municipal town can be proud of. Then why should anyone migrate to any district headquarters?

Migration to Gulf or Middle East is completely different from that to other lands of dreams, like countries situated in the West of the world. Here not only professionals like doctors, engineers, techies, teachers, officers, traders or business class, even skilled and unskilled labourers and all those engaged in all sorts of odd jobs can make a difference with their efficiency, skill, stamina, patience and other faculties- *this explains why there are more than 50 lakh NRIs (Non-Resident Indians) from the whole country in Gulf region.* Such a prospect jacked the rural economy up as unskilled and skilled labourers, who make up 55 percent of Gulf NRIs, have their roots in A-grade, B-grade, C-grade village towns and municipal towns. There is no permanent residential status in this land of immense opportunities, today or tomorrow or day after tomorrow one has to wind up the affairs. Then there is no second thought; work as hard as possible, earn as much as you can and make the base at your home village as sound and strong as possible. In those days, Gulf NRI remittance had shot up to the astronomical figure of Rs 8,000 crore. Those good old days are no more now. The rise in demand for labour pushed up the rate of migration, not only from India, but also other countries in Asia. Such a scenario brought the wages down, not the lure of Middle East. Anyway, the NRI remittance to Kerala has come as down as Rs 4,000 crore since, if I am correct in my guess, 2000. Still the lure and migration continue though it is not as lucrative or beneficial as before.

I will always remember Gulf boom for the positive impact it had brought on the state and its citizens. It fired up the psyche of the state and consequently self-belief, self-esteem, self-confidence, self-respect and above all, ambition that Keralites are noted for! 'If you or he can, why can't I' attitude got immense boost and the daring and dashing Malayali went as far as he could with his exceptionally high degree of adaptability and accommodation. He can't help it because he lives in a society which demands, 'be rich and

89

earn respect.' Definitely, education has a charm here, but add to it money or wealth, it is all the more best!

I will always credit that phase with the beginning of an economic boom. A boom that ended up in individual as well as the state's progress, irrespective of upper or lower castes, forward or backward classes, religion, region or any nook and corner of the state. That is how it happens when you are obsessed with the thought that you are in a land of no opportunities. You are then obliged to create opportunities lest you lose feet and fall down. That is when the bait in the form of self-employment descended from nowhere. With the funds that the government doled out in the form of loans, the money he could accumulate by way of his familial sources, other means and the awareness that the Left movement had inculcated in his mind, Malayali went for a kill. None, upper or lower castes, forward or backward classes, religions or regions, men or women were left behind in this survival race of the fittest. (Self-employment is one of the chief sources of employment here. If you have money at your disposal, this is the best place for you to race ahead in life.)

As if this was not enough, Gulf NRIs too dumped their power and pelf in the form of shops, hypermarkets, huge showrooms, medium business outlets, malls, jewellery showrooms, small shops, small and medium-size banks, etc. in all grades of panchayat towns, municipal towns and cities. NRKs (Non-Resident Keralites) too were not behind in their enthusiasm. As per reports doing round here, NRK remittance is not that bad; minimum 30 percent of their earnings may be flowing to Kerala. Many of the software barons, who created a sensation in the economic circle in Kerala, are NRKs with their base in Bangalore.

Who is Interested in Manufacturing Units?

Nobody is inclined to set up any production or manufacturing units here, because they are in the know about the astronomical wage structure in comparison to other states. It is in the range from minimum Rs 400 to Rs 1,000, sometimes even Rs 1,200 per day, for the whole gamut of daily-wagers covering farm labourers, hotel employees, construction workers, carpenters, masons, shop salesmen, mall employees, etc. (If you opt for a migrant labour, only Rs 200 could be deducted, but then I have heard employers lament over the quality of work). Who will then dare to plunge into that option of production unit even on a small scale?

That is why you can scarcely find any square in the whole state without auto-rickshaws or any transport facility of that mode. That is the reason why every panchayat, A-grade or B-grade or C-grade, has a township, comprising even up to 300 shops to cater to the needs of its citizens; some are even bigger than that. Here you can see supermarkets and hypermarkets, now there are talks of malls too. If anybody has enough money at his disposal and wishes to invest it, he will not straightaway board a bus to the district headquarters or a municipal town. The guy will opt for his village town or the immediate vicinity of his house, set up a firm there, retail or wholesale, and ensure that business in that particular area does not scatter out of his limit and improve his prospects. And it is for nothing that there is a computer institute in every 5-kilometre distance and with the privatization of education, villages and towns have enough number of educational institutions to accommodate its citizens. So a Keralite, spending his whole life in a village, need not go to his district headquarters or any municipal towns to enjoy life with education and entertainment, because he has everything within his 10 square kilometre or 10 square mile neighbourhood! Even 'used cars for sale' facility!

Contrary to what normally happens, especially in other states, it is heard that when real estate prices, all types of inflation and other fiscal crunches hit the roof, some people from cities shift their base to municipal and village towns in the hope of better advantages in life. Maybe, this is showing an upward trend. Let us hope this migration in 'opposite' direction will only balance the ratio between urban and rural population as well as real estate prices!

No Low Density of Population in Villages!

When there is no migration from rural to urban areas, where is the question of a low density of population! I cannot visualize a panchayat with a population figure of less than 20,000. Supposing there are, that may be in the loosely populated Wayanad and Idukki districts, the youngest and the hilliest. As everybody knows, there are world famous tourist destinations like Thekkady, Munnar, Adimaly, Kumily etc., in Idduki district and Mananthawadi, Sulthan Bethery, Kalpetta, etc., in Wayanad district. Even if the pockets of population are a little distance apart, the connectivity via road and communication facilities should not be lacking, considering the scale of development that the state has witnessed. Normal population in a panchayat would be in the range of 25,000 to 45,000 in view of the density of population of over 900 people that the state has recorded.

Needless to say, with a high density of population, the Panchayati Raj System or the local body governance is the best run in the country and any concerned ministry of any form of government of any party will vouch for it. In fact, many a minister has lauded Kerala's achievement in this department. The delivery system in the state may not be perfect or 100 percent foolproof with complete utilization of funds, meant for developmental projects in panchayats, but without the least doubt, I can assert that normally 70 percent are put to proper use. Just the opposite of what happens in other states!

This is Urbanization Dear!

This is quite understandable and visible from the appearance of these panchayats. Not only motorable roads and panchayat highways, even those meant for pedestrians (they may not be bus routes), are asphalted. Such constructive strategies like this may sometimes culminate in new routes and roads. Lined along the fringes of these motorable and pedestrians' roads and panchayat highways are well-planned, well-designed, well- crafted and well-sculpted houses or palace-like structures of minimum 2,500 square feet, hemmed in on all sides or surrounded by lusty greenery. Beautifully painted in bright and light shades with touches and strokes of magnificence and brilliance, these majestic structures can be seen concealed in thick foliage of trees with their stems and branches spread out in all directions, then flowering, decorative and well-manicured bush-like plants. That marvellous sight may have prompted the World Bank officials to state that villages are vanishing in Kerala! What to say, even Subhash Palekar, main proponent of Zero-Budget Nature Farming and a native of Amravati, was astonished and exclaimed to my cousin, a naturopath, "Are these what you call villages? No sir, these are to be called towns or urban centres!" Which means they have already acquired the look and style of urban centres. This is what I will define as urbanisation.

That is the Power of Education!

That is the power of education. As a Bollywood superstar once stated, "See what Kerala has achieved with the power of its educational credentials; none of the other states are near it, that too without any 'great' industrialization." The seeds of a comprehensive education was scattered and sown around 1,300 years ago, exactly speaking in the 8th century during the spiritual odyssey that the great Adi Sankara undertook from Kalady, his birthplace in Kerala, to Kailas to restore the fading glory of Sanatan Dharma or Hinduism. Near every temple that he monitored in Kerala, Sankara ensured the establishment of a Vedic school. The trend went on its way unhindered, though it had a casteist twist as only upper castes were entitled to that privilege. Then during the later stages of last millennium, came Christian missionaries with carrot in one hand and cross in the other to propagate the teachings of Jesus Christ. The best means they employed for conversion was education and they established academic institutions, which later turned into embodiments of repute and glory. In fact, they might be the brains behind English education in the country. That trend is continuing even today and education has been pivotal in stimulating ambition, self-belief, self-confidence, self-esteem, self-respect and many such psychological faculties that assist in the overall development of an individual.

Apart from these, social reformers, representing various groups like Dalits, Ezhavas, Nayars, etc. awakened the sense of dignity, self-esteem, self-respect, etc. in the respective communities. The state that was pilloried as a 'lunatic asylum' by great Swami Vivekananda, because of its inhuman and nauseating social customs and practices, had to declare Harijan Temple Entry in 1921. That path-breaking reform itself kindled the self-esteem of the community, which had been trodden and stamped down by stifling suppression and untouchability. These are the reasons why Kerala produced the first Dalit President and the first Dalit Chief Justice of India in K R Narayanan and K G Balakrishnan respectively.

Now the question of diverting funds by the arbitrary intervention of certain regional Titans, who think they are more equal than others, to their areas of influence and control or fiefdoms: I do not think it is possible in a state, where coalition ministry or 'collusion for the spoils' by various parties of different ideologies from different regions has become an immutable norm. Even if it happens, the issue is likely to end up in an 'assemblyquake' with unimaginable and obscene ramifications like fisticuffs, strippings, throwing of slippers and sometimes even 'mutual opening up of private parts.'

Then the chauvinistic pampering or unjustified promotion of a particular region: again this is a distant possibility where every citizen values his panchayat or municipality or corporation the most. What else is needed to stir a hornet's nest!

None can dare to ignore agriculture! Can the state government be deaf to the grievances from agriculture sector, especially the cash-rich cash-crop farmers, who have been testing their luck with coconut, rubber, ginger, spices like pepper (previously, it was known as 'black gold' in most of the countries in the world and Kerala has always been the front-runner in its production and export), cardamom, cinnamon, nutmeg, cloves, fruits like pineapple and a lot more crops? Not the least.

Now I think banana crop too has caught everybody's fancy and business eyes and you can witness its presence in plenty at all fields and compounds across the whole state.

Coconut has lost its monetary lure due to the disease that caused its massive degradation in quality across the state, then occasional dip in rubber prices and above all, the resultant decrease in flow of money to the market; all these prove the impact that cash-crop farmers can create on the state's economy. These developments do not drive them to suicide (but it has happened some years back in Wayanad district like a chain reaction), instead inspire to become stronger as they have MPs and MLAs, who dance according to their tunes. The subsequent pressure is reflected in the dust that these people's representatives kick up in Assembly and Parliament. Undoubtedly my dear, it is people who develop a nation.

So education has taught a Keralite to think with his head rather than heart. He has also been enlightened with the truth that development or progress by means of all facilities, both civic and social, is not the gift of his MLA or MP or local body representative. He knows, instead, it is his fundamental right as the citizen of this country. He is ready for only one compromise: 'Okay, no issue, let politicians fill their pockets, but first they must fill our stomachs and pockets'!

Manufacturing or Production is the only Industry?

I have read reports of Kerala Chief Ministers being 'juggled' by mediapersons for the state's alleged repelling attitude towards industrialists (reference here is to manufacturing or production sector) and recklessness of its workforce in resorting to frequent strikes to press their demands.

To my mind, it appears that there is no fun in trying to conquer the whole number of zones of productivity that lie sprawling in the horizon of opportunities; it is better if you choose to exploit the possibility that suits you the best.

I do not deny the recklessness of workforce, but it is stupid to expect that every Keralite will exposé himself to all kinds of exploitations in his homeland, that too before outsiders, interested only in cheap labour! Even before insiders they don't do that!

This is the land where many of daily wagers, including masons, carpenters, painters, small-scale unit workers, farm labourers, head-load workers and all others, whom we categorise as blue-collared professionals, zip or zoom or whiz up and down for work and familial responsibilities on Heros, Hondas, Suzukis, Pulsars, scooters and even cars. Here these daily-wagers, especially those entrusted with house construction, are pampered with breakfast, sumptuous meals, tea and snacks, besides their wages ranging from Rs 800 to even Rs 1,500 per day, so that the assigned task is executed with perfection. Believe it or not! You have to deposit lakhs for a head-loader's job here!

A climb-down in the demand for hefty wages will be well and good!

One thing is for sure: countries and human beings have to adapt to pulse of time to survive or pull on. Pulse of time in any era is not going to adjust to their idiosyncrasies. Today, there is a Gulf region or the West to thrive on. Tomorrow saturation may put an end to that dream. So what? Then another Gulf region or possibility may resurrect from the unknown depths of time and they will have to jump on to that for survival and progress. It is better not to think about tomorrow too much for, as Jesus Christ has said, "Tomorrow will take care of itself."

The 'voracious' trade sector: I don't think there is any need to elaborate on trade sector, arguably the highest employment-provider in the state. This is quite clear from the last chapter in Part-1.

Buoyant health sector: Kerala has a buoyant health sector. Definitely, Allopathy system of medicine has deepened its roots in the state in the form of government hospitals in corporations, municipal towns and all grades of panchayat towns, private hospitals and clinics, run by individual doctors and groups, and great many laboratories and speciality centres. And it is not looking back, rather galloping ahead because of its 'quick relief,' though its therapies are not striking favourable chord with patients due to their inefficacy when it comes to the curing phase.

That does not mean Ayurveda system of medicine is limping behind. It has expedited its system of operation by venturing into the production-cum-treatment zone. Some of the *Acharyas* have started modernizing their infrastructural facilities! For the identical reason, the state, which has nurtured and preserved its basics from very ancient times through the diligent efforts of great many *munis, maharshis and* indigenous *vaidyars* and by means of exclusive herbal preparations, remedies, formulations and even the huge wealth of aromatic plants for centuries and even millennia- now, BAMS (Bachelor of Ayurvedic Medicine and Surgery) doctors and traditional experts have taken over- is now teeming with hospitals, clinics, vaidyasalas, etc. run by both the government and private players. They draw international patients in hundreds and thousands, besides the Allopathic failures that cross over for a better and effective treatment. The rate of growth, registered by Ayurveda medical shops, has already overtaken that of allopathic category. Homoeopathic system of medicine too has started making its presence felt. Which in effect implies that opportunities for aspiring employees as doctors, male and female therapists, nurses and several other designations are on the rise.

Remarkable construction and real estate: Construction and real estate, inseparably linked and mutually coordinated as it involves buying and selling of land and after construction buildings too, is another sector remarkable for its stunning growth and display of exceptional entrepreneurship. In corporations or cities, you can stand agape at skyscrapers, dazzling multi-storeyed apartment and villa blocks, luxurious stand-alone villas that mesmerize you with their floral and lush green background and cost you crores and more, multiplexes and malls that accommodate a great variety of fabulous-looking commercial establishments, offices, theatre screens, etc. with their cool, immaculately spotless and spick and span ambience and so many other marvellous constructions and structures, designed and created by billions-worth groups like DLF, Confident and others of repute and recognition.

In municipal towns and all grades of panchayat towns, situation, texture of buildings, mode of construction and everything that is worth a note are completely different. You may or may not bump into skyscrapers or huge and imposing apartment blocks or magnificent multiplexes as 'vertical development' freaks hope for in similar lines with Mumbai. No big guns to monitor this commercial extravaganza that stretches from one end to the other in this 'karela-shaped' state. Individuals, that too enterprising ones with a little education-from SSLC to maximum diploma in engineering-and more ambition, intelligence, cunning, perseverance, etc. are the kings. I know one diploma-holder in civil engineering from a C-grade panchayat town, who never bothered to sell his talent and time to a multi-national company and so ventured into the real estate and construction zone. Now, he creates designs and models in his laptop for several qualified and unqualified contractors and sub-contractors, even ensures construction of houses of different sizes, modes, rates and other parameters, depending on the monetary worth of his clients, not for chicken feed returns. So that is the gist of the matter here! A great number of youngsters or even middle-aged persons with a SSLC certificate or diploma or degree certificate in engineering, or none of these, dabble in this lucrative sector. They may be contractors, sub-contractors, designers etc., with own masons, carpenters and labourers at their beck and call. They buy or create models, plans and designs, according to the specifications preferred by their clients, and erect fabulous and palatial houses, shopping complexes, supermarkets, hypermarkets, etc. and sell them.

Just visualize the tremendous potential for those willing to earn a living at the sweat of their brow or brawn or brain!

The omnipresent banking sector: Then comes the omnipresent (present everywhere) banking sector with its wings spread on all sides, tentacles meandering through the thick and thin of cities, municipal towns, village towns, remote nooks and corners etc. of the state and helping hands outstretched for any form of help, assistance, alleviations and mitigations. Of course, nationalized banks of all grades and scheduled banks of all capacities are contributing their bit to the financial might of individuals, establishments and even state bodies. Interspersed among these giants are the cooperative banks affiliated to panchayats, municipalities and corporations that create or work wonders with their multi-faceted operations. Flush and brimming with funds- it is heard that a considerably large chunk of Kerala's black money flows as deposits to these coffers- they run supermarkets, hypermarkets, medical shops and a variety of business options and multiply their revenue. There is a talk of even malls now! Some of the bigger non-banking financial corporations like Muthoot and Manappuram have pride of place at the national scene.

Then there are, even smaller in size and utility, the chit funds or kurie companies or financiers as they are known- earlier they had earned the notoriety enough to be nick-named as 'blade companies.' They too are branching out and spreading their outreach. They are helpful to small shops, small enterprises and even ordinary citizens, with an extra penchant to enhance their bank balance and wealth, in the form of short-term loans and kuries that would be recovered through daily collections.

Terrific hospitality sector: What should I talk about the hospitality sector? These hotels, restaurants, resorts, star hotels, haunts, outlets, etc. are all the way across the length and breadth of the state. Even if you are going to fix a diagonal direction, there too its presence is visible in the same measure and quantity. It is as if Malayalis are determined to eat it out rather than relish their homely delicacies.

This sector has begun outsourcing their responsibilities. Previously, all the snacks that you get to tuck into used to be prepared or cooked by hotel employees only. Those good old days are gone now. In what can be termed as another source of indirect employment, Individuals, in their attempt to create opportunities, have taken over and carry out that task with their own staff.

As a consolation for jobless people, another group crept into this sector, the catering bandwagon. In fact, this sector has already snatched the wedding potential from hotels, which used to carry out that huge task efficiently and satisfactorily.

If my memory is anything to go by, according to the report of one of the reputed English channels in India in 2000, Kerala used to spend Rs 1,000 crore on marriage itself every year. It is 2016 now and that amount might have doubled or trebled, even at the moment I am authoring this book. And just think that around three quarters of that market have been grabbed by these enterprising individuals and their units and wonder at the wave they have created and are creating presently in Kerala. Employment potential is more than encouraging.

Stunning education sector: I can talk about education sector with more authority as I had been out of my home state for about 27 years and was astonished to perceive the difference created by privatization of education. Unfortunately, the left leanings of the state had always played a role in that negative bias against privatisation. At last, sense prevailed over and that is reflected in the number of educational institutions that have sprung up all over. Even the villages which hadn't had an educational institution in my schooldays, that is about 45 years back, now flaunt not only schools in English and language medium, but even engineering colleges. Every morning I am witness to the college buses and school buses zipping past most of the state, panchayat and national highways. Private players include as usual all Christian Churches, religious and social organizations and even opulent individuals.

The following fact, which I am going to relate, will convince the reader that quality of education will be taken care of in this land of Adi Sankara! During the time when school teachers in the whole state went on strike, 10 or 15 years back, educated parents of students had to take over that responsibility lest their offsprings would miss out on several portions of the syllabus. Their sensibility was active despite the fact that they do not have to shell out fees in government-aided schools. So alert are the parents, more should be their sons and daughters!

It is in this state, known for its education, that the notorious case $0 + 0 + 0 = 425$ (the boy in question, that too son of a famous allopathic doctor in Kochi, did not appear for Secondary School Leaving Certificate (SSLC) examination that year, still he scored 425 marks, means he passed with distinction grade, when the result was out. How? Black hands of corruption played a detectable role) took place and it generated protests, agitations and outcries so much so that the government and departments concerned had to implement necessary nullifying measures! Such malpractises raise their heads frequently, but the beauty is that it does not take 15 years for the public or intellectuals to get a smell of them by virtue of a nosey and sharp media, always keen to bring to light such nefarious activities.

The great tourism industry: Oh, Kerala's great tourism industry, the only sector that experts are ready to grant an emphatic industry status! Its potential and performance have been hailed by many national and international experts. According to National Geographic channel, God's Own Country is one of the 50 must-see destinations in the world. Another channel dares to declare it as one of the 10 paradises in the world. And the foreign exchange that this sector brings in is deemed to have crossed the Rs 1,000 crore mark- maybe, this is an old figure. Its houseboats, backwaters, the lusty and picturesque greenery, monsoon tourism offerings, tree-top tourism offerings, Venice of the East Alleppey, Queen of Arabian Sea Kochi, etc. are major attractions. Not only that, this 'industrially backward state' with 14 districts and 3.33 crore population count has 4 international airports (the 4th one Kannur International Airport will be opened soon) at its disposal and can make use of them to their fullest potential and stimulate the sector further for more money in foreign exchange and popularity.

IT sector is waking up: The key that paves way for digitalisation of operations and functions, Information Technology or IT, has now woken up from its initial slumber, because of the scepticism that had shrouded the state's initiative for opening up itself for industrialization.

Trivandrum Techno Park is the second largest of that kind in Asia. Kochi Info-Park has wide opened its gates and doors for multi-national and Indian players in the field to exercise their sway! Many more are sprouting here and there, even in A-grade village towns. According to a reliable source, sooner or later, each district can be proud of having at least two info-parks. Already, the state is contributing 30 percent of the software professionals to India's Silicon Valley, Bangaluru. Even if they are by-passed, the state has more than enough professionals in its arsenal to stand out from rest of the states, calling shots at present.

The entertainment extravaganza: Then entertainment sector is on a triumphal note. You can just imagine the potential in a state with the highest percentage of media presence and cable TV channels playing a pivotal role. With 50 channels, that too in a language (Malayalam) spoken by only 4 crore people in the world, it is anybody's guess as to the number of programmes, serials, soaps, skits, comedy slots, all sorts of time-killing stuff, etc., the scope for creativity, advertisement and the consequential trade and employment potential.

Why to talk about media sector! Malayala Manorama is among the three highest circulated dailies in the country with a circulation of about 25 lakh copies. The two front-runners-Malayala Manorama and Mathrubhumi- have already grabbed two-third of readership in the state and 1.60 crore readers are under their control!

The huge transport sector: This is the situation in Kerala right now:14 districts, located within the reach of each other and linked or accessible to each other by way of an intricate network of roads, flyovers, bridges- small and big- transport and communication facilities. Will there be an inaccessible village then? How is it possible when there is a massive number of private and KSRTC buses at the state's and its people's convenience?

In my opinion, the total number of private buses, plying and linking villages, towns and cities, should be at least 10,000 with the addition of KSRTC or government-owned vehicles. Attach with this the number of inter-state buses. Lots of them are there for commuters' comfortable travel!

Earlier, taxi-cars used to be main mode of transport during marriage occasions. As they are highly expensive in terms of rent and can accommodate only less number of travellers, buses, which cater to the needs of tourism industry, have taken over this task too. Now you can see luxurious, air-conditioned, hi-tech and even ordinary buses zooming across all kinds of highways with marriage participants in a joyful and celebrating mood by way of fun and music.

To my mind it seems that there should be minimum 50,000 employees, with very high remuneration, serving this sector as drivers, conductors and cleaners.

It may boomerang: Even if you suppose, as the media wish, Kerala is ready to embrace manufacturing or production industry, some other sector may lose its lustre. There will be all sorts of cries of varying decibel from all quarters of the state with regard to environmental degradation, bio-diversity variation, pollution etc.. These factors will, in all possibility, toss the vibrant tourism industry in all directions and become another headache for the government. This in effect may affect hospitality sector, already at its lively best! It is better if you choose the right one that suits you the best. There is no point in gaining anything at the cost of another.

What did the state achieve with all these positive developments? A lot! If my humble knowledge is to be relied, Kerala stands tallest in 30 indicators, which include those related to economic development, social development and human development (the state tops most of the indicators and in some it is among the topmost claimants). Of course, it has the highest quality of life and standard of living!

Nuclear Family Set-up Should Get the Credit!

In my opinion, the transformation of Kerala society from joint to nuclear family mode has played an overwhelming role in the economic 'outburst' that this state has been witnessing since 70s, of course, irrespective of the occasional swing downwards as cash-crop prices like those of mainly rubber, then spices and coconuts crash. I think joint family system itself is an 'escape route' since it provides an 'elbow room' for the most diplomatic or the least enterprising among siblings, who believe, to an extent, in earning a living at the sweat of others' brow. Individual ambition or aspiration bears a heavy beating, when it comes to the crunch as collective ambition or aspiration exercises its vice-like grip. Age becomes the yardstick and the younger ones are forced to make a tactful or disappointing retreat. This in turn affects the overall boost in family's economic prospects.

Yes, sure, in a joint family, it is a festive air when it is all smiles and happiness. Real nature of members will come out only when the question of sharing grief, poverty and bankruptcy arises. I do not think life is such a senseless sharing of negative aspects.

In a nuclear set-up, with your wife and children, it is a small and comfortable zone and your creativity or innovativity or enterprise is likely to smash around in all ways and directions, making a huge difference. Here too you have the scope for emotional chill-out, but with limited number of dear ones, but then hypocrisy or the artificial behavioural tactics are rare.

I know one family, living just opposite to my house in the village. If that example is the trend for the future, joint family system is really welcome. There are about 8 brothers, who live in a land or compound of, say, 5 to 6 acres. Each sibling owns a house, built as per his monetary power. Each one with his wife and children sweats it out on his own. The benefits from the compound or land are shared by all. If anybody is in fiscal straits, others may or may not come to his help or rescue. Anyway, individual talent does not get misused or suppressed, at the same time the emotional relief from mutual sharing of happiness and sorrows exists. This case is the rarest of all rarities!

Some of the votaries of joint family system-in most of the states, this is still the custom-may assert that it is family and not individual the most important. Then it is same as Communism's motto: individual is subservient to state.

So, I assert joint family is a Communistic set-up and nuclear family, a democratic set-up!

Black Spots of God's Own Country!

This Lure and Migration has no Sense!

Why this lure of and the migration to Gulf, though it is not as lucrative or beneficial as before, continues? Gulf NRI will thunder, "Kerala is a land of no opportunities." Not at all! Opportunity is an option that can be created if you have the will to do so by shedding your inhibitions like false prestige. I consider this as a grave problem which has infected not only the state of Kerala, but the whole country. A 'prejudiced' Indian believes in 'dignity of labour' only when he is outside his home state; which means he is ready to do any, even odd jobs, because none of his friends and relatives are at the spot to observe or disdain him.

I think no nation can bring the process called development to its logical conclusion without respecting and practising the mantra called 'dignity of labour.' Nowadays, I have observed several Keralites practicing that mantra in the compound or land, adjoining his home by grappling with the soil with spade or any agricultural implement, watering the plants and vegetables he cultivates, spreading manure or cow dung around their roots, etc. Well and good, though he is not ready to earn a living here in such a manner!

My point is that if you can do it outside your homeland, why can't that be so at home! If that 'disdainful' look is the culprit, then it is time to nurture sense of self-respect and sense of self-esteem, because opportunities outside the state and the Gulf region are not an eternal option. Saturation is hovering over these prospects; today or tomorrow or day after tomorrow, you will have to fly back home. In Kerala, today the wage structure is equally good as in Gulf or even better and far higher than in other states.

This reminds me of another strange habit among Keralites! Many of them are not prepared to work any odd jobs at home. Take for example the job of a salesman in a small shop. The normal wage is Rs 300 to Rs 500 per day. He will not be willing to do that job in Kerala, but in Maharashtra or Tamil Nadu he will do it for Rs 100 or Rs 200 respectively, because that is the norm there. When you are in Rome, you have no other option except to do as Romans. In Nagpur, in 2004, a mason used to get Rs 150 per day and in Kochi, the wage was Rs 750 during the same period. You can almost make out the basic difference in wage structure between both the states.

Thus, on a fine morning or day, when they reach home because of saturation of opportunities by way of nationalization or localization of jobs due to immense pressure from 'sons of soil' votaries, Keralites from Gulf will find migrant labour at every junction and spot in the state, making the best use of the chances available. What will they do then! Can they make use of their exceptionally high adaptability and accommodation and survive by getting rid of all prejudices? Many of the earlier Gulf returnees had chosen business as the alternative. Everybody may not be in a position to follow that line for lack of financial resources.

See the 'Hole' in Education!

Education has definitely played a stellar role in the economic revolution that Kerala has been experiencing. There is an axiom in Ayurveda system of medicine, which reads like this: in excess, even medicine can be poisonous! Education too has such a problematic aspect. This is quite evident from what is happening in India's most educated state. Education has not left out any caste or creed or religion or even panchayats of any grade in its unfettered advance.

So, offsprings of carpenters, masons, goldsmiths, ironsmiths, toddy-tappers, Dalits, etc. are no exception. You will find doctors, engineers, graduates, post-graduates and other technically qualified people among them. The problem is that many of these professionals are not ready to opt for the traditional work, come what may, even if they are jobless. They consider it as infra dig (below their dignity).

Actually, they are not to be blamed. "You know, my dear son, I am educating you because I do not want you to do the menial job that I am doing now. So take care and make the best use of this opportunity and get a white-collar job, so that you can hold your head high in dignity and walk," is the advice that their parents usually hammer down into their head, right from boyhood. From scratch itself, they might have developed a kind of contempt for this traditional work. Not only that, peers and even neighbours provoke them with nasty comments like this: "Don't you have shame to do this job with a degree in hand." This is the reason why there is a huge shortage of such professionals here and migrant labour from UP, West Bengal, Orissa, Tamil Nadu, Chhattisgarh, Jharkhand and Bihar are taking advantage of those golden opportunities. There are complaints about the quality of work, but I think time will rectify that anomaly!

Anyway, the consolation is that several students, especially those hailing from lower middle-class and poor families, are ready to earn some money for their educational purposes by choosing part-time jobs. I know one Standard X student, who works in a chicken shop on his weekly holidays-Saturday and Sunday. This will fetch him Rs 4,000 or Rs 4,500 a month, depending on the number of holidays he works. Then there is one ITI (a technical course) student, who works in a vegetable outlet on weekly holidays and earns Rs 2,400 a month. They utilize the money for their education and don't have to extend their hand before their parents for fees!

The trend is spreading wide and finding favour with college students too. It is heard that some of them, pursuing Plus Two, Degree, Post Graduation and even technical courses, are doing part-time jobs so that they don't have to rely on parents for fees.

Thank God, of late, Gulf returnees have started putting the typical Keralite's high degree of adaptability and accommodation into practice in his homeland. The job of a hotel waiter normally does not carry much weight or status in our country. In short, it is treated as a blue-collar job. Certain Gulf returnees have no problem with that and are bucking the trend. For them Gulf and Kerala are the same. In a recently inaugurated hotel in the nearby town, most of the waiters are Gulf returnees. We can guess that sense is prevailing over Keralites outside and hope this trend will catch up with others, who are likely to pack up soon. Why only waiter's, every job has got its own status!

Let us hope dignity of labour is taking root and making its presence felt just as in the West!

My Goodness, Water Scarcity in Wet Kerala!

What is this scarcity or shortage of water in a state that receives an average 300 cm rainfall every year? Incredible! That should not have happened if Keralites had opted for conservation long back! The way this precious and cheap source was being squandered is unpardonable. I still remember, during my college days when dark and thunderous clouds would split open and gush out in torrents, nobody would bother to raise a small barricade in his area of land, small or big, in order to prevent whole quantity of rainwater from flowing to drain. That small barricade could have conserved that much quantity, enough to increase the groundwater level.

The reckless reclamation of paddy fields, lying as if they are virgin lands, mindless consumption of sand from rivers (even before the advent of April and May, the rivers get dried up and remain wide open for children to enjoy the game of cricket till monsoon sets in and raindrops start their lashing-spree!) and merciless deforestation or destruction of nature-all in favour of real estate sharks for generating millions and billions- have contributed to this disastrous situation. (My passionate assertion about destruction of nature in this spiceland will surprise outsiders, especially tourists, domestic and foreign, because for them-in comparison it is true- Kerala is still the greenest state in the country!)

What and where are we up to? Will myself, on the threshold of senior citizenship, be unfortunate enough to witness Latur-like situation in this God's Own Country: hundreds and thousands, devastated by drought and with parched throats, flocking to cities and towns to quench their thirst for water and life? Or will myself be part of those brigades, running helter-skelter and racing after drinking water tankers, for buckets of water like in Mumbai?

Already, global warming is taking its toll by scaling up the temperature to sweltering level! Even seasonal rainclouds hesitate to open up and pour out here!

Stop this Consumption of Poisonous Vegetable!

More than 60 percent of essential commodities that Keralites consume are imported from other states like Tamil Nadu, Andhra Pradesh, Telengana and Karnataka. Actually, what is the need for such massive imports, when fertile lands lie sprawling at your disposal for discreet utilisation? Another proof for an irresponsible attitude on part of a state and its people, pretending to be wallowing in the problem of plenty!

The following pathetic situation is with regard to vegetables. They are mainly imported from Tamil Nadu, where farmers cultivate vegetables well in advance with an eye on Kerala market and preserve them using banned poisonous chemicals. When the time is up, straightaway, they despatch them to Kerala without any sort of purification. Unsuspecting customers here buy and consume them.

(If a Malayali and a snake are seen at a time, flog the former first for he is more poisonous than the latter-so goes a common saying in Tamil! Now you decide who is more venomous!)

However, media's sharp eye and nose succeeded in detecting the menace. The whole hell broke loose from all corners of the state in the form of vehement protests and awareness campaigns. Even the Malayalam movie 'How old are you' contributed teeth to this campaign by highlighting the dangers of 'polluted' vegetables and advantages of 'pure' vegetables, cultivated at home without the help of any chemicals and fertilizers. Now, according to a survey, import from Tamil Nadu has come down by 30 percent. This is no time to be complacent and people here should continue cultivation at home so that they and me can consume pure and 'chemicalless' vegetables. Same outlook in the case of paddy too will be beneficial.

No home-Made Snacks, only Bakery-Made Ones!

I think my sense of taste has lost the flavour of home-made snacks that we used to enjoy during Christian feasts and Hindu festival days. Each Christian feast, for that matter even Hindu festival, has its own snack specialities and they would be prepared at home by the coordinated efforts of family members, kith and kin. With the warmth created by those get-togethers, the snacks would be extremely tasty. Nowadays, with the advent of nuclear families that mutual love and affection (though artificial) is missing, so too are these home-made snacks. Here again Malayali is affected by the plenty syndrome!

Gradually, individuals or families, armed with a penchant or inclination to create opportunities, took over the preparation of these snacks and started supplying them directly to bakeries and hotels. Once their availability in bakeries spread like wildfire among families in cities, municipal towns and village towns, housewives hung the devices and gadgets they would use for the preparation. Now, we buy these snacks from bakeries and hotels only, but that flavour, spiced with love and affection of family members, kith and kin, is gone forever!

Is this the Health that we Hail or Laud!

One of the aspects that makes this state a cut above the rest is its achievements related to health. When the country has a doctor-patient ratio of 1:1,000, Kerala's corresponding ratio is 1:200; really a vast difference. However, the truth is that Kerala has proportionately the highest number of cancer, diabetic, cardiac and other patients. This is the greatest paradox: Kerala is healthy, but Keralites are unhealthy! Strange! I think our definition of health has to be changed. Is it not strange that the healthiest state has proportionately the highest number of patients, doctors and hospitals? If the state is really healthy, it should proportionately have the least number of hospitals, doctors and patients!

This spotlights the truth that the medical warning, 'prevention is better than cure,' has lost its relevance long back! Now the trend is to eat, drink and make merry for we have enough doctors, hospitals and medical facilities at our disposal! It also highlights the 'over-indulgence' that the most educated state has become 'notorious' for!

So, citizens and comrades, no complacency, smugness or even jingoism! Remember those four lines of Robert Frost which can wake you up from the slumber called complacency:

Woods are lovely, dark and deep,

But I have promises to keep,

And miles to go before I sleep,

And miles to go before I sleep.

www.ingramcontent.com/pod-product-compliance
Lightning Source LLC
Chambersburg PA
CBHW051319220526
45468CB00004B/1410